# Bread of Angels

# Bread of Angels

## Patti Smith

BLOOMSBURY PUBLISHING
LONDON · OXFORD · NEW YORK · NEW DELHI · SYDNEY

BLOOMSBURY PUBLISHING
Bloomsbury Publishing Plc
50 Bedford Square, London, WC1B 3DP, UK
Bloomsbury Publishing Ireland Limited,
29 Earlsfort Terrace, Dublin 2, D02 AY28, Ireland

BLOOMSBURY, BLOOMSBURY PUBLISHING and the Diana logo
are trademarks of Bloomsbury Publishing Plc

First published in 2025 in the US by Random House, an imprint
of Penguin Random House
First published in Great Britain 2025

A catalogue record for this book is available from the British Library

ISBN: HB: 978-1-4088-6772-3; TPB: 978-1-4088-6773-0; EBOOK: 978-1-4088-6775-4

2 4 6 8 10 9 7 5 3 1

Typeset by Six Red Marbles India
Printed and bound in Great Britain by Clays Ltd, Elcograf S.p.A

To find out more about our authors and books visit www.bloomsbury.com
and sign up for our newsletters
For product-safety-related questions contact productsafety@bloomsbury.com

*Obstacles are our wings.*

NIKOLAI GOGOL

# Contents

# Bread of Angels

# Prelude

THE PEN SCRATCHES across the page *rebel hump rebel hump rebel hump*. What do these words mean, asks the pen. I don't know, replies the wrist. These are the words forming and the writer, stationed at Dolina Charlotty, in a valley in northern Poland will decide later. Charlotty, a name evoking the porcelain face of a doll, left in the grass by a child so that she might go off to pick wild berries. Not for very long, yet long enough to be forgotten, and through the passing of time the abandoned doll becomes Charlotty in the rain, Charlotty in the snow, Charlotty pulled apart by a playful dog. Her porcelain head swathed in the shadows of beech trees growing higher through seasons of snow, of red then dead leaves. Seasons of sun fade the pink of her cheeks yet fail to subdue the impassive intensity of her marble eyes.

Why a porcelain face? Why not a rag doll, such as my own, with button eyes on a face of cloth? This penchant for alluding to things I never had, where does it come from? This unaccountable attraction to the so-called finer things described in books: a linen waistcoat, kid gloves, soft leather boots.

Combing through pages, as if imagined steamer trunks, for one velvet cloak, a dress to disguise the miniature Quasimodo trapped inside an awkward child's body. My rebel hump, my unbecoming yet altogether necessary rebel hump.

Laying down my pen, I find myself humming a melody of long ago, a song of the swampy woodland where I once lingered beneath fast-moving clouds, beguiled by everything. Rebel hump rebel hump, tramping through the reeds, the uncompromising ferns, sidestepping the stinkweed and swarms of gnats and mosquitoes. There I tied a small hammer to my belt, together with a miniature flashlight. I cracked open rocks searching for their secret hearts, signaled for alien ships to take me far afield and waited patiently, willing to embark. I removed my shoes, followed streams laced with algae and rushing tadpoles, on alert for the glint of a certain coin that afforded entrance to the underworld. Or the jagged edge of a shard that when placed at an exact point would connect with corresponding fragments, fashioning the hand mirror of oneself, an ivory one at that.

I leave my work behind and enter the forest surrounding Charlotty, inspecting internal mechanisms of the oldest of trees. Encased in the concentric rings of growth are the fibers of four white dresses, the living cells of childhood. The starched folds of a Communion dress. The fragile remnants of the dress of art. A party dress, delicate as a handkerchief, possessing the upright naivete of rock and roll, given to me by my brother. Lastly, a pristine Victorian tea gown, my wedding dress, embodying vows and tears shed for my husband, whom I loved for a time more than myself.

God whispers through a crease in the wallpaper, a drop of water bursting as an equation. Light in the forest falls. An old man sits on a barrel singing, *I found a gold coin in a field, who will change it for me?* A child calls out to him. *Maybe my doll when I find her. She has a purse filled with silver.* By will alone, a doll materializes. Charlotty. First an arm then a torso then a small proud head whose fixed blue stare has witnessed the casting out of the seraphim and the burning of the reverberating stars.

Everyone is dead, all is forgotten, echoes a voice. I inventory those still with me. I go no further than the face of my sister, innocent yet all knowing. So long as she is here our memories are ensured. But what of the future when we are both gone? Write for that future, says the pen, for the sake of the cast-off lamb, swept away as ash in a burning attic. The hourglass overturns. Each grain a word that erupts into a thousand more, the first and last moments of every living thing.

I see myself on tiptoe reaching for a crimson book, the object of a toddler's greedy curiosity. I wanted to know what was inside, and in time desired to write one myself. I believed I could write the longest book in the world, record the events of every single day. I would write it all down in such a way that everyone would find something of themselves. Some might stay with me, others take wing. For my part, I would spew from the edges of a radiant mound illuminated by the rays of a punishing sun, a singular traveler in search of the garden of childhood's hour.

# The Age of Reason

THE FIRST SENSATION I remember is movement, my arm waves back and forth, a small endeavor that results in the toppling of Bugs Bunny from my highchair tray. My silent partner, propped there before me big as life, disappeared like a Viking ship tumbling off the edge of the world. All but a blur well beyond my reach; the earliest consequence of an action. I remember being held by my father and how different it felt from being held by my mother. He was calm; I sought his reassuring shoulder. I gravitated toward him though it was my mother who was ever present, ever dominant. Not yet one, I took my faltering first steps across the kitchen floor, then kept going. My mother was continuously challenged by her inquisitive and mobile first child who could not resist exploring, disengaging from her grip, breaking free in the park, disappearing in department stores, and spurning her affection.

She warned me of the cost of a thousand actions, but I had to see for myself and was thus bitten, stung, and exposed to all manner of insults and injuries. With little sense of the

*Memorial Day, 1947, Chicago*

struggles surrounding me or the havoc I caused, I'd reach for the forbidden, a lit cigarette, a silver table lighter, flicking it to produce a pretty flame, sliding a tight rubber band on my wrist. A burned finger, a blue hand.

Bit by bit I piece together an ever-expanding mosaic of my pre-existence. At the end of World War II, Grant Harrison Smith, emotionally broken and plagued with malaria-induced migraines, returned to Philadelphia from active duty in New Guinea and the Philippines. He never graduated from high school, instead joining his sister and brother as the principal dancer in their tap and acrobatic trio, but the war had cut short their prospects. Beverly Williams, a young widow who had lost a son in childbirth, was working in a nightclub. They had known each other as teenagers and found comfort and familiarity in one another after the war. He was uncertain about the times ahead but believed television was the wave of the future. In 1946, he applied and was accepted to a technical school in Chicago that included a postwar incentive of a twenty-dollar-a-week stipend. Following his plan, my parents wed in a simple civil ceremony and boarded a train to Chicago. They rented two rooms in a boardinghouse in a Polish neighborhood near Logan Square. My mother, pregnant with me, worked as a waitress for as long as she could stay on her feet.

I was due on New Year's Eve, but arrived in the center of a huge blizzard, a day early, ruining my mother's opportunity to receive a promotional New Year's gift of an early freezer prototype. Instead, she continued using an old-fashioned ice chest, waiting each week for the iceman in his horse cart to deliver a large block of ice.

Within the pages of *My First Seven Years,* my oversized faded pink baby book filled with lists of illnesses, birthdays, and notations of my progress, my mother inscribed a poem entitled *Patti.* One could sense her joy giving birth to a little girl, though a sickly one with severe bronchial distress. My father said I was born coughing. He bundled me up, and together they departed the hospital in a swirl of snow. My mother said that he saved my life, holding me for hours over a steaming stand-up washtub. But I knew nothing of these things, neither the hopes of my father nor the labors of my mother, soon pregnant with another child.

My sister Linda was born thirteen months after me, during yet another Chicago blizzard. At two, I couldn't pronounce Linda, so I called her Dinny, and for some time that name remained. I can picture my mother with her dark wavy hair and ever-present cigarette, with me toddling about, another in a carriage, and secretly carrying a third beneath an oversized Chesterfield coat. When she could no longer hide the pregnancy, our landlord forced us to relocate. With a third child on the way, my father was obliged to leave behind his vision of stepping into the fast-evolving technical world of television and find full-time work.

My mother listed all our addresses in my baby book. In the first four years of my life, we relocated eleven times, from rooming houses to furnished flats. We traveled by train to Philadelphia, stopping for a brief, unwelcomed stay with my father's beautiful but mean-spirited sister, Gloria. I can picture my grandmother Jessie's spinet, a small upright piano, and my aunt whacking me for attempting to play.

That winter we moved from Gloria's to nearby Hamilton Street. My father found a job in a union factory, working the night shift; my mother continued to waitress. On Christmas Eve after a long day waiting tables, before she boarded the crowded bus home, my mother bought two large lollipops and two small hand-painted wooden penguins for our stockings, all she could afford. When she got off a strap dangled; someone had cut it and made off with her shoulder bag. She would recount the story over the years, still stricken that we had no presents for Christmas that year. Since then, I have found it impossible to pass up little penguins in flea markets or dime stores, as if to fill the vast ice field left in her sad sturdy heart.

Our new baby brother was born in June of 1949. He was named Todd, a small, wrinkled thing wrapped in a pale blue blanket. My mother set him in a wicker bassinet, and we were told not to disturb him. I remember standing over him staring, overcome with the sense that he needed protecting.

Soon after I was diagnosed with tuberculosis, spreading among poor immigrant children in our neighborhood. To safeguard the little ones and offer me a healthier environment, my maternal grandfather, who we called Daddy Frank, spirited me from our crowded Philadelphia rooming house to his sheep farm in Chattanooga. He was handsome, good natured, and played ragtime-style piano. I was free to run in the fresh air and fattened on sheep's milk, along with heavy doses of streptomycin administered by a large glass hypodermic. I would later learn Daddy Frank's much younger and childless second wife Dolly had it in her mind to keep me.

My mother loved her father, but after nearly a year of

separation, she was forced to legally threaten him to bring me home. She said I returned with a Southern accent, patent leather shoes, and a silver fork and spoon set with PATTI LEE engraved. I have little recollection of this estranged stretch of time. My baby book only contains the date of my flight to Chattanooga and a blank page for how we celebrated my third birthday.

On May Day 1950, we moved less than two miles away, across the Schuylkill River, to Baring Street. I was talkative and rambunctious, so my mother allowed me to perch on the stoop by myself while the baby slept, so long as I promised to stay put. I was happy there observing the last vestiges of the 1940s, soon to succumb to modern times. There were horse-drawn wagons, the iceman, a ragman, and an organ grinder with a monkey with a little red cap. Across the way was a medieval-style building, built in 1892 by an Irish railroad baron. It resembled a small castle with crenellated towers, a Victorian wood porch, and a gabled roof. It was later transformed into a Dominican House of Retreat, a fairy-tale place manned by scurrying friars in black cloaks over white robes. The comings and goings on Baring Street fueled my imagination; the storybook castle and the organ grinder's friendly monkey found their way into future tales I would weave for my siblings.

Linda was quiet, much smaller than me with big, astonished eyes, always tagging behind holding on to my dress. She had a sad-looking doll named Jessica. It must have been a secondhand doll, or born in poor condition, but she loved Jessica and dragged her everywhere. One day one of Jessica's arms came off. I desperately tried to fix it, but the rubber band attaching the little arm had snapped. Her arm sat on a shelf waiting for a more capable surgeon.

My mother now had the three of us to tend to. She taught us our prayers and policed the precious arena of my lively imagination. She noted in my baby book that I was prone to falsehoods. If the truth didn't interest me, I presented an alternative reality. To curb my skilled little mind, I received some whacks from the paddle, along with futile attempts to guide my early Bible study and moral education. She had little time to field my endless metaphysical questions about Jesus and the angels and the ins and outs of heavenly bodies. Recorded in my baby book in her hurried script are two of my questions: *What is the soul? What color is it?*

I plagued my mother with so many questions during evening prayers she decided to enroll me in the Presbyterian Sunday school. At three and a half, I joined the older children memorizing scriptures. I was content for the time being though none of my questions were answered. At bedtime, I would recite what I learned to Linda, who listened wide-eyed with her one-armed doll in her lap.

Toddy was a sickly baby, and we treaded softly so he could sleep. One night I awoke from a nightmare in which I was playing with the baby, perhaps too roughly, and pulled off one of his tiny arms. I woke sweating, unable to distinguish reality from dream. I felt around in the dark for Jessica's arm, lying in state on our dresser, and rushed to the bassinet to attach it. He began to cry, and my mother found me half asleep poking him with the doll's arm. She was furious with me. I had frightened her and disturbed the baby. I returned to bed confused and strangely haunted by the experience. For years this nightmare would return, always the same sequence. I would see myself in the pajamas that I had already outgrown, the uneven cut of my thick dark hair, my hand outstretched holding the doll's arm, whispering my brother's name: *Toddy.*

My mother had been able to hide her pregnancy from the new landlord, but not a crying infant. We were uprooted yet again and temporarily moved back with Aunt Gloria on Rambo Terrace where we lasted for three uncomfortable months amid the inhospitable atmosphere and dark wood paneling. I still desperately wanted to touch the keys of my grandmother's glowing spinet. The instrument had been left to my father; my mother promised that I could have it when we had our own home and counseled me to be patient. My father's mother, Jessie, died of cancer on Palm Sunday several months before I was born. She was a gentle lace maker who played both spinet and harp, one of six sisters whose family emigrated from Liverpool in 1890. My father loved his mother deeply and often said Linda's empathetic nature had its roots in her. Jessie faithfully kept diaries, one for every year, mostly recording the weather and family activities. When I got older, I often tried to imitate her daily practice but would forget for a swiftly passing succession of days.

On May 6, 1951, we moved to Newhall Street, a temporary arrangement offered to families of soldiers as they searched for more stable living quarters. It was a whitewashed complex with a barracks feel, consisting of three attached two-story buildings each housing four families. It overlooked a wide unkempt field sprinkled with daisies and dandelions; the whole compound was affectionately called the Patch.

Directly behind us was a concrete area with overflowing trash bins, oil barrels, rusted cans, and discarded junk. Often, with no adults on patrol, we would assemble there searching for treasure. The massive crawl space beneath the buildings was called the Rat House. Poorly boarded up, it was the forbidden core of the complex, and we explored it with our pocket flashlights. It was dark, dusty, and dotted with the red eyes of large city rats. These were our playgrounds, one humming with nature, the other with debris, equally esteemed by the neighborhood children.

At four years old I had more freedom to explore than my siblings. Toddy was yet a toddler. Linda seemed born to sit among the wildflowers surrounded by butterflies. Instead, she sat in the dirt in the back of our tenement housing, innocently regarding the clouds above, oblivious to the scurrying rats and the mud seeping into her cuffed socks.

We lived on the second floor of the first building across the hall from an old Jewish man and his granddaughter, sole survivors of their family. He worked in Klein's Chocolate factory, wore a heavy black coat, and was cautious and soft-spoken. My mother shared our fare with them, and he would extract a large rectangle of chocolate from the folds of his overcoat. At night my mother, always a sympathetic listener, sat with him in the kitchen. The little girl with dark eyes never said a word, never seemed to let go of his hand, and after a few months they quietly left, as did others, without saying goodbye.

We saw many immigrants come and go, but the core group, mostly families of servicemen in economic limbo, shared resources and watched out for one another's children. On hot summer nights, the grown-ups would convene in lawn chairs, smoking cigarettes, drinking dandelion wine or a Seagram's and soda. The men talked of the war, women revealed secrets to one another, kids ran wild. After six months, all the tenants received an eviction notice followed by a series of demolition postponements that allowed us to stay for nearly four years, providing our first real sense of home. Most of the families were relieved by the continuing reprieves, dreading the next lap. The ever-present question hanging in the balance: Where would we all go? Perhaps a relocation shelter, or a smaller apartment, or a temporary stop in yet another condemned building. As our parents grappled with an uncertain fate, we practiced oblivion—the future was a grown-up concern. We children had our own trials with rats and bullies and tick-infested dogs and a surfeit of illnesses to negotiate, in our own cruel yet magical reality.

In months to come I badgered my mother about the spinet, though clearly there was no room for it in our small apart-ment. Gloria had put most of my grandmother's belongings in storage. My parents didn't have the money to pay the storage bill and eventually lost everything, including the spinet, the English china, and my father's boyhood books and sled. This came as a great disappointment, and it pained me that it would fall in the hands of a stranger. I can still see my outstretched fingers trying to reach the ivory keys.

Jessie's green brocade sleeper sofa was saved, and it

dominated the living room that opened into a small kitchen lorded over by a potbellied coal stove. We all loved that old-fashioned, oversized couch. On special occasions or during a big storm, the three of us would wash together in the tub, put on our pajamas while our mother opened it up and we'd scramble in and share a big bowl of popcorn. The green couch remained a comforting haven through the years, connecting us with the grandmother we never knew.

My mother's younger brother Bobby often visited us, usually bearing gifts. He gave us small matching dolls, pink bunting for the girls and blue for the boy. Toddy wanted the pink one and I wanted the blue, so we secretly traded. He was very attached to the pink dolly and one afternoon while playing outside he dropped her, and she tumbled down a small cliff. He tugged at my shirt in tears and led me to the spot. I could see her halfway down, caught in some brambles. They both stood in expectant silence as I assessed the situation. I saw my task and determined the best route. Shimmying down, I held on to the jutting rocks, grabbed the dolly, and pulled myself back up with just a few scratches.

Linda, as Dinny the nurse, picked bits of dirt and prickles out of dolly's bunting. The gratitude in Toddy's face was heartbreaking. They were both so small and barely talked yet seemed strangely wise. We shared an inexplicable telepathy. A language all its own, manifesting most deeply in our Game of Knobs, melding the truth of imagination and our common ability to be as one mind. Sentenced to silence in our room for some childhood crime, we discovered a perfect way to communicate. We would sit before an old maple bureau with two

*Siblings, the Patch, 1951*

knobs on each drawer, some slightly loose, and wait until the perfect moment. Then I would give a nod, and we'd close our eyes and turn the knobs in unison. Effortlessly we'd board our small ship with sails made of threadbare sheets, suddenly luminous, and we were off. The sea of possibilities we sailed in would be forever our own. Not making a single sound, not a hoot or an enchanted exclamation, as we flew through a spectrum of blues, greens, and variants of red, rose and gold and silver, a Crayola Box of crayons.

My mother became close with an Irish Catholic family who lived directly beneath us. Mary and Les, their three sons, and Aggie, their great-grandmother. Mary had been bitten by a huge rat as a child and had a deep scar shaped like a ring of teeth on her neck. The neighborhood kids feared and respected Aggie, but I was fascinated by her. I had never known either of my grandmothers, as both died before I was born. Aggie was bedridden and would happily read stories to me. My mother scolded me for bothering her, but Aggie shooed her away explaining that she had all the time in the world. I have only one memory of Aggie getting out of bed, so tiny, under five foot, in a pale nightgown with a long white braid trailing loosely down her back. She rummaged about, finally finding *Irish Fairy Tales,* a dark green book stamped in gold with a warrior raising a shield, flanked by two hunting dogs. She indulged me by rereading my favorite passages. When she dozed, I would play with a few soldiers I kept in my pocket. Her quilt was my field, her poor swollen stomach was my mountain.

I missed seeing her for several days when I came down with the measles. When I got better, I entered the quiet apartment as I always did, without knocking. The door was never locked and Aggie never left so I fully expected to find her there. I was hoping she would read to me but upon entering her room, everything was gone: all her things, her soft patched quilt and the magical green book. No one thought to tell me that Aggie had died while I was sick. Back then children were seldom told anything. I stood there wondering what to do, then sat quietly in the chair where I'd always sat and envisioned my soldiers sliding down Aggie's quilted mountain.

Recently reminiscing with Linda, I spoke wistfully of Aggie, describing her book of Irish fairy tales, lamenting that I no longer remembered my favorite passages. Some weeks later, I received a mysterious package in the mail. No card, no words, just as my mother had often done. A green book stamped in gold, the same warrior raising a shield. At first, I could hardly bear to open it, then took a breath and eagerly read of the boyhood of Fionn, recognizing the passages I had once loved. *All desires save one are fleeting, but that one lasts forever.* That was the desire for wisdom, which Fionn wholeheartedly embraced, and when asked what he would do with wisdom he exclaimed, *I would make a poem.* Reading this passage, I recalled Aggie's Irish brogue, her trembling hands, and the fire of my imagination.

When it was time for kindergarten, leaving my siblings behind was painful but I was also curious about school. With no bus service, I walked a mile and a half by myself from the Patch to Charles W. Henry School, a historic two-story

red-brick colonial on Carpenter Lane. I walked along the highway, crossing the bridge over the Schuylkill River, once called
*Tulpehane,* or Turtle River by the Lenape. In high winds I feared
being swept away and in heavy rain arrived home drenched,
possibly the cause for reoccurring bouts of bronchitis. But I
loved the magnificent turreted structures in the distance, so different from the abandoned structures in our condemned neighborhood. I'd develop long-running stories of a pauper child who
found favor with a king, until I arrived at school and climbed
the steep limestone steps through the wide arched door.

At some point I found a shortcut through a small wooded
area. On certain mornings I would stop and linger by its pic-
turesque pond. The sun played on the surface so dazzling
that I was certain it was a dwelling place of spirits, a pocket
of paradise. I loved this secret haven tucked away from the
busy boulevard. It was there I discovered a very old snapping
turtle. Back then there were many snapping turtles in the
Philadelphia area. People caught them to sell to restaurants for
turtle soup. One morning he climbed slowly from the pond's
shallow edge and stopped just a few feet from me. I sat on a
rock clutching my red plaid school bag, mesmerized. He was
massive, with ancient eyes, surely a king. We communed just
as I had with my siblings in our telepathic play. I entered his
world, though I could hardly say where we went. It seemed
to last only a few moments, but when I arrived at school, my
teacher was very angry; it was lunchtime, I had been gone all
morning.

My mother had been in a state of hysteria as she had a mor-
bid fear of kidnapping, haunted by the death of the Lindbergh

baby. She was relieved and furious, grilling me in every possible way, trying to comprehend where I had been. I could only answer *nowhere,* for it would have been impossible to explain. She remained so upset that my father intervened, suggesting we take a walk. He asked me to show him my nowhere. I led him through the shortcut, past the playground, and he held my hand as we entered the wood. Everything was still. He sat on the rock with me, and I confessed that I had been talking with a giant tortoise. He asked me a few more questions, and then we sat happily in silence, a rare moment that I have often revisited. I wished he could have seen the turtle, but he didn't surface again. When we walked back, I asked him if he would tell my mother. I will tell her you are fine, just daydreaming as you are prone to do, and you lost track of time. We can keep the rest between us. My father never said another word about it. My mother scolded me for taking a different route, making me promise not to do it again. That night, I felt that all was well, but said a little prayer for the king of tortoises, sadly knowing I would never see him again.

My mother took in ironing with a woman from work named Novella, for five dollars a basket that they split equally. One Saturday, Novella took me and her son to the zoo. She took both our hands, and we walked along eating cotton candy. I had never held her hand, which was big and soft, when I noticed something new. Aunt Novella, I said, why is your hand darker than mine. Well, I don't know, honey, she laughed, it's just how God made me. And that was that. Soon after we passed a fortune teller who caught my eye and hissed at me. Pay her no mind, said Novella. But it worried me, it seemed like a bad sign. But why did she do that? Novella stopped, bent down, and smiled. Because you're special, she said, don't ever doubt that.

Despite being scolded for straying I continued to explore whenever possible. Around Halloween, I ventured out to look at the roller skates that I had spied the week before in the window of Pep Boys. There was a shortcut through a stone tunnel that emptied out onto Wissahickon Avenue, declared out of bounds by my mother. The clouds had moved, blocking the sun, and the entrance was a bit dark. I hesitated, but the sun broke through, and a burst of light illuminated the exit at the other end. There I caught a glimpse of tiny jewels, scattered treasure across the path. Rubies, topaz, and perhaps a few emeralds, glinting then disappearing into newly formed shadows. Images of the Seven Dwarves mining barrels full of jewels and singing heigh-ho, flashed before me. I stood transfixed, frozen, then swiftly formulated a plan. I would gather the treasure, rescue my family and neighbors from poverty, pay all their bills. I would buy the skates, and Linda and Toddy could have anything they wanted. It all happened in seconds. I rushed toward the jewels then halted. On the ground before me were hundreds of M&M's, red, yellow, green; my rubies, topaz, and emeralds laid bare in a shaft of sunlight. I had never seen so many M&M's. I picked them up, wiped them clean on my shirtsleeves, and filled my pockets. Normally I would have been elated to find so much free candy, but I felt tricked, a victim of my own innocent illusions. I ate the M&M's in a state of defiant grief, all of them, failing to save some to share with my siblings.

I was not present at my fifth birthday party. Instead, I laid in the dark, stricken with a severe migraine, though not as horrible as my mother's, and was consoled by the thought that I was likely suffering a malaria headache like my father. The following morning, I found a package from my mother on the kitchen table, the ball-bearing skates from Pep Boys that I secretly coveted. She always seemed to know what I was thinking, what I was up to, good or bad. She scrutinized my movements, could easily spot a falsehood, grilling me constantly, causing me to hide truths that needed no hiding. It was our greatest source of conflict. She desperately tried to keep track, even shape me, but I stubbornly remained outside the mold. Yet she was also able to determine what was vital to me. I loved my skates, they were exactly the ones I wished for and can still access the thrill of strapping them on, tightening them with my skate key, and feeling the surface vibrations as I speedily skated on forbidden boulevards.

Kindergarten was disappointing, sitting in a circle chanting from Mother Goose, learning by rote, curling on joined desks to take a nap. My legs were too long, and I was much too restless to sleep. I suspect I was regarded a doleful child, a bit of a loner, I have little recollection of interacting with my teacher or schoolmates. I preferred the company of my siblings and exploring my own thoughts, however abstract, until I gradually developed the language to express them. And that language was poetry.

Mine was a Proustian childhood, one of intermittent quarantine and convalescence. During my first six years I weathered one communicable disease after another, bronchial pneumonia, tuberculosis, German measles, mumps, and chicken pox. After the first stages of each assault, I would enter periods of lengthy bed rest, lying in my makeshift cot by the coal stove, picturing the characters in my books, spinning them adventures beyond the page. Nothing induced horror in me more than an oversized glass hypodermic emerging from a doctor's black bag. I would attempt as long as possible to conceal symptoms of impinging sickness, frequently consulting the tattered remains of *The New Family Herbal; or, Domestic Physician,* a guidebook of medicinal herbs and natural remedies inherited from my mother's maternal grandfather who practiced country medicine. The frontispiece showed two guardian angels. Fragile, wrapped in cloth, it languished on our bookshelf. In my mother's absence I would unwrap it and try to decipher its contents, which sometimes crumbled at the touch. I was determined to save myself and my siblings from the dreaded syringe thick with penicillin.

I studied the descriptions of diseases at the back of the book, then searched for corresponding natural remedies. An infusion of freshly picked dandelion leaves, or lemon and honey, or apple cider vinegar were surefire curatives for minor afflictions. Toddy was too young to be plagued with such concerns. Linda was my ally. When she and I came down with symptoms of an unknown illness, fever, chills and runny noses, I turned to the natural bible and diagnosed diphtheria. After downing an extra spoonful of vinegar, we immediately got into bed, covered our heads with blankets and successfully sweated out whatever we were temporarily suffering from. Linda and I still happily share our secret medicinal bond; we had conquered the dreaded diphtheria on our own.

Though illness was an ongoing companion, I did not identify with the bedridden in books. Mary Lennox in *The Secret
Garden* was my role model, a scrappy orphan who survived the
cholera that claimed her family yet urged her guardian's
wheelchair bound son to walk. I discovered that Robert Louis
Stevenson and L. Frank Baum had been bedridden as children
and prevailed, strengthened through the power of their mon-
strously beautiful imaginations.

I believed that my own will coupled with natural remedies
kept me alive. I was too young to appreciate that my well-
being was more likely due to the care bestowed on me by others. My father saved me as an infant. Despite her heavy
workload, my mother sat bedside when I was felled by illness.
Only years later, and certainly after her death, was I able to
fully grasp her sacrifices and comprehend her complicated
emotions.

My mother existed most of her life without a mother's love.
My grandmother Marguerite died before I was born. She was
small, green-eyed, high-spirited, and played the mandolin. My
mother adored her, but she tragically had a psychotic break,
became violent, was institutionalized in 1932, and never came
home. She no longer recognized her children yet was always
loved and yearned for. Their once happy musical household
crumbled, and my mother and her two younger brothers were
deposited with their grandmother Olive Lily Hart, who had
raised four sons and welcomed the little boys but was cold and
indifferent toward her.

My mother was never able to permeate the hard-hearted
Olive, who everyone called Grammie. A tall, formidable

woman from the Midwest who wore a cameo broach and skirts to the floor. She was a descendent of British dissenters, rode a horse, and raised her own siblings when abandoned by her widowed father. Someone I would have happily romanticized, but she displayed the same lack of affection for me as she did my mother. I watched as my mother scrubbed Grammie's laundry on a washboard, rinsed and hung it to dry, then folded each piece, filling a large basket, without eliciting a single word of gratitude. On one such visit, as we said goodbye, Grammie took a large jar of hard candy out of a glass cabinet and offered it to my siblings, but snapped the lid shut when I reached for one. My mother stood there in silence; I took her hand and said nothing.

That night, before she tucked me in, my mother gave me *Silver Pennies,* a precious book of poetry, one of the few cherished remnants of her childhood. I understood the significance of this book and solemnly accepted it. We didn't speak of Grammie's strange behavior nor the candy nor the laundry. For some things we needed no words.

The slightly battered *Silver Pennies* was lovingly given at a time of unfettered curiosity, without instruction, save to believe. I mulled over the book's opening line: *You must have a silver penny to get into Fairyland. But silver pennies are hard to find.* I was certain that within this little book I would find the entrance into the mystical world I most desired. I labored over the poems and memorized a prayer to the elves and fairies, the mischievous angels of earth. *God and the Fairies, be true, be true! I am the child who waits for you.* I repeated it to myself as I walked to school.

I reckoned that finding a silver penny required a two-pronged strategy. The heart to pierce other dimensions, the eyes to observe without judgment. One may be obliged to draw out the protectors of the small kingdom who kept the pennies in their store or seize the wings of a fairy and barter. I pressed my hand against the soil, feeling for the vibrations of their tiny feet. I kept my eye to the ground in search of shining strays, only visible when caught in a certain light. I also considered the possibility of earning a silver penny but was unable to penetrate some of the more enigmatic verses. I awarded my favorites with penciled stars, giving the most to W. B. Yeats's poem *He Wishes for the Cloths of Heaven*. The desire to understand them motivated me to accelerate my reading skills, which I accomplished with my mother's tutelage.

In time I would come to realize that I already possessed my pennies. In lieu of a specific coin, I had something even more precious. My mother had given it to me and her mother had given it to her. The small volume was the storehouse, and the poems were the pennies. Poetry, the wondrous language much prized by the young warrior Fionn, formed a map that led to the kingdom of the infinite imagination.

I couldn't wait to go to grade school, which I had envisioned as freedom, including an unlimited access to a library stocked with children's books. I was free of the watchful eye of my mother only to be placed under the rule of a stern and forbidding teacher. We spent the first tedious months reading *Fun with Dick and Jane,* featuring their dog Spot and Zeke the philosophic gardener. I sped through it and was often discovered reading a book of my own choosing during class. When asked questions, my mind would be elsewhere. I was made to stand, bewildered, looking down at my feet. Your feet won't have the answer, my teacher reprimanded.

My one joy was setting out our tools for penmanship hour: a Carter's glass inkwell, another small bottle of the allotted ink, an institutional-issue dipping pen, and three nibs in a plain blue matchbox. The desk had a hole on the right-hand side where the inkwell poorly fitted, causing several mishaps. My desktop was stained with Rorschach blots of those who preceded me. In my earnest labors, I soon added my own mark with droplets of ink spotting the wood, smudging fingers and the edges of my sleeves. I loved completing the exercises at my small desk. The sun pouring through the wide, high windows spread patches of light on the worn planks of the uneven floor. I often found myself gazing up at these windows during reading and mathematics lessons, lost in unformed thoughts, but not during penmanship hour. I couldn't wait to write in cursive. I can still picture my schoolmates, their heads bowed over horizontal sheets of lined paper, their pens scratching in unison. I would join in the chorus, forming the loops and curves that would one day become letters, then a string of words. I had watched my father fill out his checks and so admired his elegant backstroke that I later practiced his signature on canceled checks, over and over.

In the schoolyard everything seemed to push me further in a corner observing others. No longer the leader of my trusted army I stood by myself around the perimeter. It was there I overheard my teacher whisper to another that I was an odd duck, as if let loose from a Hans Christian Andersen tale. I was out of step and yet in my mind several steps beyond, for I brought back the worlds I had feverishly dwelled in, read, or created.

None at school suspected that I had a dual identity, the unspoken leader of our small neighborhood gang. I had modeled myself after the cartoon character Little Lulu, who lived in a world with no adults. She was my guide, mischievous, yet principled and independent, with a sense of responsibility to the young. Like her, I told stories, designed our play, drew maps, made elaborate strategies for imagined battles, and enforced our boot camp drills. We called ourselves the Buddy Gang, with our own secret passwords and calls. We played the games our parents had played: Spinning Statues, Simon Says, Red Rover, but preferred the games and battles of our collective imagination. Medieval knights with cardboard swords sheathed in tinfoil and trash can lids for shields. Winter war games conducted in bunkers of heavily packed snow, homemade maps, and impossible missions. The wounded bandaged, the enemy forgiven. As General I was then left alone to contemplate the morrow's maneuvers.

Most Sundays after Bible school, decked in Wranglers and red plaid shirt, I would conduct my routine search through the trash. Ever the scavenger, I found two stacks of *Vogue* and *Harper's Bazaar* tied with red string. I stuffed the string in my back pocket and designated the oversized magazines for scissoring clothes and accessories for Linda's paper dolls. I had always used my mother's discarded Sears catalog. Transfixed, I quickly realized these were no Sears catalogs. I noticed the same woman appeared from issue to issue exuding a confidence that I admired. I placed a Sears catalog alongside *Vogue,* and compared the two presentations, from the commonplace to the transcendent. What made them different? I sought an answer to explain my deep affinity to the *Vogue* images.

I found myself musing on the way one might carry oneself, composed, aloof, self-assured. Subconsciously, I absorbed the work of some of the great contemporary photographers: Penn. Horst. Beaton. Frances McLaughlin. It was an intuitive kinship. These early issues of high fashion magazines, which I continued to study throughout my youth, made an indelible mark, introducing me to the world of art, photography, style, and an ever-expanding aesthetic vocabulary. Years later I identified the model who had so intrigued me to be the sculptress Lisa Fonssagrives-Penn, the image of intelligence and grace.

In the streets surrounding the Patch were several boarded-up houses. I was drawn to one set back in a medium-sized yard overgrown with high dry grass, Queen Anne's lace, and slim stalks that I imagined to be wheat. The smaller windows were broken, the path to the bolted door was completely overrun and it was said to be infested with rodents, massive spiders, and the dust of webs. I was standing before it after a rain, entranced by the play of light on the yard and the mottled façade. Just a small insignificant house with a ragged yard, yet it appeared mystical, silvery, holy. There were two coins in my pocket, allotted for penny candy. Fingering them, I was overcome by a strange presentiment. A waving veil lifted, and a mathematical formula came to life aided by spirits: The pennies would return one day as gold in the palms of my hands. I tossed my coins into the abandoned yard, certain no one would find them, neither the curious nor the vandal. After that day, I tossed every penny I received into that forlorn little yard. Every cent represented the sacrifice of a miniature Tootsie Roll, a spearmint jelly, or a stick of licorice. Though I loved candy, I invested my coins in my distant future. Through my life I have envisioned that forgotten yard, hundreds of pennies illuminated, a child's fortune strewn.

January was the coldest month in Philadelphia; my sixth birthday was celebrated with the chicken pox which spread quickly among us, three spotted dominoes falling one after another. When we all recovered, we joined our mother on a series of coal missions. We'd follow her down by the railroad tracks. We loved waving to the conductor as the coal cars passed. Then we'd collect pieces of fallen coal in our baskets to feed the kitchen's potbellied stove, our sole source of heat. On one such cold afternoon, gathering coal, my mother's lively black cocker spaniel ran on the track before us and was struck by the oncoming train, killing her instantly. We stood in shocked silence, then did our best to comfort our weeping mother. We trudged back home in the snow on that wintery Sunday to get a fire going and bury her black dog.

Death and disappearance were synonymous. First Aggie disappeared, my mother's dog, and then a little boy on the first floor named Dana Kitchen. He was barely four and died of cancer. His family held a wake for him in their apartment; he was dressed in a grey suit with a bow tie. The grown-ups all convened in the living room. We were allowed to watch Saturday cartoons in the room where Dana was laid out in his coffin. We pushed the TV closer to Dana and sat in a circle. And then he was gone.

Not long after, I was down with the mumps. I spent my time in bed reading *Peter and Wendy*. This book suited my dual nature. Like Peter Pan, the provocative leader, I never wanted to grow up, content in planning impossible escapades, yet I also felt an affinity with the introspective Wendy, the lost boys' Scheherazade. I found myself torn between intoxicating solitude and my impatience to get back to my scrawny gang who counted on me, especially when faced with Jackie Riley, the universally feared neighborhood bully.

Jackie Riley was big boned with bright red hair and an equally fiery temper. He was often on the prowl with his gang preying on the small. Toddy, barely four, trembled at the sight of him. One Saturday, after cartoons, my gang was set to meet behind the Rat House. The little ones, continually under my protection, headed out, but my mother had one of her debilitating migraines and I was recruited as always to take care of her. These migraines could last for hours through day into night, obliging me to stay rooted by her side. Hastily, I applied Bengay, cold rags to her forehead, placed a bucket by her bed, and skipped out as soon as possible.

I raced downstairs and ran the length of our barracks to join my comrades. Turning the corner, I heard a familiar cry. Toddy was in the grip of the enemy, who was shaking him and laughing hysterically. All the members of our camp, surrounded by Jackie's gang, quivered. There was no way I could beat Jackie Riley, who was much stronger than me. I was about fifteen feet away and swiftly surveyed the situation. He had a very prominent vaccination scab on his right arm. I spied a piece of sharp slate among the stones. I kept my eye on his naked arm and let the slate fly, spinning in his direction. The slate miraculously found its mark, slicing the scab from his skin sending streams of blood down his freckled arm. Toddy broke free, the jeering ceased, and Jackie Riley ran off howling for his mother.

It was a shining moment hardly equaled in my young life. No greater accolade, no medal of honor nor proclamation of recognition could measure up to the admiring faces, not only of our tribe, but the army of our arch enemy, who joined in the cheering. I was hailed by a gaggle of scrappy kids with dirty faces, skinned knees, torn polo shirts, and homemade bowl cuts. My siblings walked proudly by my side as we headed home, Toddy vowed to be forever my knight.

We were met at the top of the stairs by Mary Glasgow, hands on hips shaking her head. I rescued my brother from the hands of Jackie Riley but had failed in my duty of caring for my mother. The shades were drawn, and the apartment reeked of Bengay. Mary Glasgow took the little ones across the hall, and I was left to sit in the dark, changing rags, making ice packs and rubbing my mother's temples, indifferent to her moaning.

My mother once said I had a heart of stone. Leaders had to be tough, I would tell myself. These were the moments when I wished I could just whisk my siblings away to my own version of Neverland, away from all ties to the grown-up world. It wasn't until I was much older, felled by my own migraines, that I comprehended her suffering. My young son, without prompting, would selflessly care for me, bringing cold rags and quietly sitting by my side.

She stands in memory in all her glory, in a Communion dress and veil, vain as a lily. She was Suzanne, my nemesis, soured by privilege, with superior airs like the camel in *Just So Stories*. In the tale, the hump was a punishment for the camel's haughtiness. I believed my hump was a badge, one I would cherish and hold fast until the day it would materialize like a shimmering hologram.

Suzanne lived above us. There was a wondrous sense of community in the mix of servicemen and immigrants waiting for a GI loan or relocation instructions. But Suzanne and her father held themselves apart. They were of a different ilk, as they impatiently waited to be installed in a fine Philadelphia mansion. Though Catholic, they did not align with the struggling Irish Catholics, nor the spattering of Italian immigrants, all hurled together in limbo.

Suzanne insisted that she was there by mistake, and with her disdainful looks she never let anyone forget it. Her father brushed past us on the stairway in his cashmere overcoat, as if there was sewage on the stairs, wincing with every step. Suzanne did not join in our games, she stood on the outside like the haughty humphing camel, taunting us, imposing tasks in her service in exchange for the favor of sitting on her bike, a twenty-inch Schwinn Pixie, with coaster brakes and no training wheels, the only such bike in the neighborhood. One Saturday afternoon Suzanne conjured a fresh scheme. She challenged us to race across an abandoned lot, littered with debris and broken glass, uneven concrete with spiky weeds pushing through the cracks, some bald patches of dirt, and a few resilient dandelions. The winner granted an afternoon riding her coveted bicycle. The news of the race spread quickly. A slew of us, girls and boys, different ages, different sizes, lined up and readied ourselves. A wide cyclone fence covered in thorny bramble served as the finish line.

I was a swift runner and figured if I concentrated, I could win. It seemed an interminable wait, then just like that she raised her arm and cried, *Go!* I was off to a good start, flying past everyone, like Sacajawea in her winged moccasins. I was just a few feet from the finish when I tripped over protruding concrete. I rebounded quickly and touched the fence, blood dripping down my face, a shard of glass embedded in my brow. The other kids started screaming. For me time seemed to suspend, I had done it. I had won.

My mother took me by trolley to Children's Hospital. I was proud of my battle wound. A surgeon took pity on us after my mother admitted she had no money to pay him. He used a new technique, butterfly stitching my brow with dissolving catgut. Such a pretty girl, he said, I promise you won't have a scar. Then he gave me a patch to protect my right eye.

The following Sunday, I spotted Suzanne back from Mass. I walked up to her and another girl, both a bit older. I grabbed the bike, flipped up the kickstand, and stared them down. I'll be back in a while, I said. I had never ridden a two-wheeler bike, but I had nothing to lose. I hopped on, took deep slow breaths, and after a few teetering starts I was off. I left the perimeter of the Patch, pedaled up toward Wayne Avenue. I was six and a half years old with seven stitches, and for that one hour, on that two-wheeler, I was a champion.

Suzanne may have been guilty of cruelty, but my own transgression was possibly worse, breaking the tenth commandment, coveting my neighbor's goods. Many times, I sat across from her as she spread her worldly store on the carpeted floor. Leather-bound fairy tales, a Cinderella watch, charm bracelets, snow globes with scenes of distant places. But the most wonderful of all was a dress stored under her bed in a shiny white box. In rare moments, she would slide it out and open the lid slowly. There, within layers of tissue, beneath her Communion veil: A white dress.

The pen stops with one beat of the heart. I can still see it, white dotted silk with a satin sash, a cloud of a dress. She would let me look at it, savoring my adoration. Impulsively, I reached to touch it, forbidden as I might inadvertently soil it. Suzanne never took it fully out of the box, so I was left to envision its silhouette and the length of the hem and the veil.

It would come to me, more spirit than dress, a dove-shaped flounce of tulle. I imagined wearing it with my cardboard sword, my trash-can-lid shield. I believed it had special properties, like an invisible cloak, and that it would keep one safe from harm. With such a dress as my wispy armor I could achieve anything, truly champion my brother and sister, protect the small in the neighborhood from all outside forces. I also imagined it might have the power to transform my nemesis. Perhaps, as she walked the aisle to receive Communion, Suzanne would become a better person.

Suzanne would reach the age of reason before me. As a Catholic, she would wear the white dress and veil as she entered her new stage of life. Our family belonged to no organized religion, had no such rituals, nor religious objects, but we owned a large, illustrated family Bible that my father bought before I was born.

The day before her Communion I stood next to her in her room. I was tall for my age, but she was taller. Laid out on her bed with its pale coverlet was the white dress. Alongside it was a white rosary and a prayer book, with her name stamped in gold. Such beautiful things that I could not help but desire much to her delight. Suzanne taunted me, allowing me to look but not touch. She also promised after her Communion to give me her old scapular, hanging from a brown shoestring. She would be receiving a new one on white silk. I was happy about this, for I believed that it too had special powers and looked forward to when she would press it in my eager hands.

I always believed in the magical properties of things. Before I had speech, I grasped for them. I believed there was a mystery woven in the threads of the scapular that I would solve. I imagined wearing it would augment my prayers. As always, I kept these things to myself, trying to appear indifferent.

She was the most beautiful sight I had ever seen, as she stood at the top of the stairs in her white dress. Her veil, fastened to a garland of tiny white flowers, fell to her waist. She wore white gloves and held her mother-of-pearl prayer book. As she brushed past me to go downstairs, she turned her head, stuck out her tongue, and smugly descended, haughtier than ever.

That afternoon when Suzanne returned, she tapped on our door and beckoned me to follow. Back at her apartment, she stopped in front of the refrigerator, opened the door, and extracted a jar of mayonnaise. It was well known that I had an extreme aversion to mayonnaise. She lifted a heavy silver spoon and dug into the jar, scooping out a mountain of mayonnaise and waved it in front of my face.

—If you want the scapular, she said, you have to eat it all.

I refused, and she accused me of not loving Jesus.

—Of course, I love Jesus, I protested.

—Well, if you love him, you'll eat it. That's what they gave him on the cross.

—They did not, they gave him vinegar.

We bantered back and forth until I'd had enough and left, empty-handed, while she continued to wave the spoonful of mayonnaise in the heavy air. Her father passed me on the stairs as if I was less than a ghost. I returned to our apartment. My father was listening to a ball game.

—Daddy, I said, what did the soldiers give Jesus to drink when he was on the cross?

—Vinegar, he said without hesitation, and he took the family Bible off the shelf and read me the scripture. Satisfied, I climbed back up the stairs, Bible in hand, and knocked. Suzanne opened the door, still in her white dress.

—Look, I said, it's right here. I showed her the scripture proving it was vinegar. She glared at me. I had won the argument but not the scapular.

—I threw it away, she told me, and I winced inside, imagining my undisguised want lying in a tangle in our rat-infested dump, coiled among the refuse of the day. All these things dotted the map of my young mind. I vowed to be better but feared I was marked.

Soon after, my nemesis and her fascist father exited the Patch without a goodbye or a turn of the head. Their departure was met with jeers from the neighborhood children. I noticed that their apartment door was left open, and I slipped in to scavenge anything left behind. In the kitchen was a chipped plaster saint and a pile of *Life* magazines. I took the saint but left the magazines behind. I stopped for a moment before the refrigerator. I imagined it full of jars of rancid mayonnaise. I closed the door behind me and skipped down the stairs, my rebel hump shining.

OCCASIONALLY MY FATHER would treat himself to a visit at the barber shop. We'd watch fascinated as he got a shave and a haircut. Sometimes the barber would let me sit in the chair and he would trim my bangs, always uneven by my mother's handiwork. On one such trip, we discovered a basket of shaggy puppies the barber was giving away. We were captivated with the smallest one, with the short hair of a shepherd but markings like a collie, and begged my father to let us keep her. In a moment of weakness, he acquiesced. We named her Bambi because she had a face like a deer. I became attached to her and when I was sick, she would lie at my feet.

Although often battling some new ailment, I took pride in the fact that I always recovered. But I was also aware of an older girl in our quadrant who suffered from lupus, an incurable and debilitating disease. Stephanie was bedridden, condemned to a lonely life of failed convalescence, each season growing weaker. I visited her occasionally, sitting bedside. She reminded me of Clara Sesemann, the older city girl with frail health from *Heidi*. I was certain that I could help cure Stephanie like Heidi cured Clara, but I was never able to induce her to rise from her bed or step out into the sunshine.

Her mother encouraged me to visit Stephanie more often. Her room was pretty. The shelves were lined with trophies and trinkets, a cigar box filled with charms and a jewelry box with a tiny silver key. We were always alone in her room, she wore no jewelry, her face pale, her hair braided. Sometimes she would drift to sleep, and I would sit and read her comic books. In truth it was her stack of comics that lured me, especially her complete collection of Superman.

Early one winter afternoon, while I was engaged in our child wars, I could feel Stephanie summoning me. I reluctantly left the scene of our play to visit her. She seemed weaker than ever; after a time I grew restless, eager to join the others building a snow fort in the field. Perhaps sensing my restlessness, she asked me to get her jewelry box and instructed me to unlock it. A melody played as I slowly opened it, and a small ballerina turned. Her ploy had worked, I was captivated by the contents in the velvet lined compartments. I knew right from wrong, yet that winter afternoon as she dozed while propped up on a mound of pillows, I took a pin of an ice skater from her jewelry box.

I was still sitting at the foot of the bed when she opened her eyes. I wondered if she somehow knew what I did, but she didn't say anything. She might have given it to me had I asked, instead I stole from a bedridden friend. I hadn't imagined the consequences; the debilitating waves of conscience that kept me awake at night. I continued to visit Stephanie only with growing trepidation. I kept my head down when her mother spoke to me, but no one even mentioned the pin.

Hidden beneath loose floorboards of a closet was my secret stash. Glittering refuse I had scavenged from trash bins, fragments of costume jewelry, rosary beads, clay animals from cast-off crèches, guarded over by my old blue toothbrush. I believed it was a magic brush, that communed with me as I brushed my teeth. When my mother replaced it with a new one possessing no telepathic powers, I retrieved it from the trash and set it beside the chipped plaster saint. This was where I hid the pocketed skater pin, in the dusty underworld beneath the flooring.

For my seventh birthday, December 30, 1953, my mother surprised me with our first trip together by trolley to Leary's Bookstore. It was a large three-story building with a sloped roof. Including the basement there were four floors of books and a mezzanine. The children's books were on the top floor. I proudly presented Mr. Leary with my birth certificate and gave him a dollar. It was the store's policy to let a child fill a shopping bag with books on their birthday. My mother left me there to choose my books and went to work at Strawbridge's, only a few blocks away. In those precious hours surrounded by books, I was completely alone, an entire morning of unmitigated joy. Mr. Leary came to check on me and noted my piles, where I was selecting and eliminating. You have a good eye, he said, picking up a copy of *A Christmas Carol* bound in limp green suede with Dickens's name stamped in gold. My mother returned to collect me on her lunch break. Mr. Leary said that I had chosen so many precious books he would soon go out of business, and I sheepishly offered to return half of them. Instead, he presented me with the famous Leary bookmark with a gentleman from another age on a red stepstool choosing a book.

Despite any conflicts with my mother, that day a new ritual unique to us was born, based on our common passion for books. Despite our difficulties, she maintained an attentiveness to the things that were important to me. For the rest of her life, she gave me books for my birthday, from the Bobbsey Twins to William Blake to Baudelaire. My favorite book I had chosen on that charmed afternoon was *Alice's Adventures in Wonderland*. It suited my desire for nonlinear adventure. Alice was completely relatable; I admired her spunk and independence. Having had a lengthy discussion with the tortoise king, I had no qualms concerning the validity of her lengthy sparring with forest creatures. The chapter entitled Advice from a Caterpillar gave me much to ponder.

*Who are you?* asks the Caterpillar.

Who am I? I had often asked the same of myself. I was happy with my family but could not help feeling an inherent estrangement. It was certainly not due to a lack of love. Alice searched through Wonderland and again in *Through the Looking-Glass* hoping to find a recognizable image of herself. I wondered why I seemed so different, in appearance, in temperament. I couldn't find my face in the faces of my family, which spurred sly comments from neighbors.

On rare instances when we were allowed to sit and look at my parents' collection of family pictures, I furtively sought a likeness of myself in snapshots of my grandparents, aunts, and siblings. Then one day I chanced upon something significant in a yellowed newspaper picture. A faded image of my father breaking through a ribbon, winning a race in his boyhood home of New Haven. I was also a fast runner, the fastest kid in the neighborhood. I asked my mother if I could have it and she slipped it in a little tin frame. This is why I am here, I reasoned. To break through walls, through ribbons. This is who I am, I whispered, I am you.

THE ENTRANCE INTO the age of reason comes at a price. In the wake of my seventh birthday, I came down with another bout of bronchitis. While recovering I was struck with an acute awareness of what I had done. I had stolen from a bed-bound girl; I would be free to go back outside and play but she would not. The price was the consuming conscience that the naughty and curious Pinocchio tried to escape. I had compromised innocence. This is what we yearn to reclaim, the child's purity, the realm of love. When her mother beseeched me to visit her again, I could not refuse. Stephanie was quieter and paler than ever. She fell asleep as I read her comic books, and it occurred to me that perhaps I could return the pin to the jewelry box while she was sleeping.

When Linda started attending school she was entrusted to my care, crossing the bridge over the Schuylkill River, never letting go of my hand. As winter snow swirled, we made our way holding tight to one another in fear of great gusts of wind. I couldn't bring myself to share my woes with my innocent sister. As if the sin of coveting wasn't bad enough, I had become a small thief. At night I could feel the pin's presence, as my crime gained in stature in my mind. I feared the pin would rise from the boards, a reproving figure with a flounce of a skirt and silver blades.

In the days that followed, I couldn't help but look up at Stephanie's window, imagining her calling to me. I decided to confess—instead of sneaking the pin into the box I resolved to be truthful. I waited nervously outside the Holts' door, pin in pocket. Her mother answered and I was told to come back another day. When I did, her mother, anxious and distracted, told me again that Stephanie could not receive visitors. I sullenly shuffled back; the pin, wrapped in a napkin, remained in my pocket. A few days later, after school, I tried yet again, but this time no one answered, and I left, feeling perplexed and shut out. I placed the wilting napkin with its sad contraband back beneath the floorboards. February arrived, and the groundhog saw its shadow.

I was reading Dick Tracy to my siblings, the Sunday comics spread out on the floor. In the evening the atmosphere seemed very heavy. Normally the three of us would be in the bathtub, waiting to be scrubbed by my mother, put on our pajamas, and watch the beginning of *The Ed Sullivan Show* as a family. Only that night a woman we didn't know put us to bed early. Stephanie was in the hospital and the neighbors were called upon to give their blood. My mother and father were gone a long time, and I couldn't sleep. I remember my head hurt and I had a strange otherworldly feeling. I convinced the babysitter to let me lie on the green brocade couch with a blanket while she watched television. I tried to imagine what was happening at the hospital, as I wasn't sure what giving blood entailed. *To be safe from harm,* was my new mantra; I silently chanted it for Stephanie.

I felt like a child, yet also ancient, as if a human relic from a primordial culture. I wished nothing more than to be scooped away in the palm of a magnificent genie; I'd command him to reverse time, so I could sit at the foot of Stephanie's bed, slowly open the pink and ivory jewelry box, and though hypnotized by the ballerina slowly turning, I would not run my fingers through her things, touch her watch, necklace, nor take the skating pin. I was vexed by the idea that we were condemned to dwell in linear time. If time was meaningless to God, why must we suffer it? Surely, we once had the capability to dwell otherwise, like a race of time travelers. I lay there trying to go back as far as I could remember, much further than my hands opening the lid of the jewelry box, searching for an ancient portal that most certainly existed.

When my parents returned home, it was very late, weariness their countenance, their efforts fruitless. Stephanie had fallen into a coma while my mother was giving blood, and my father, still suffering lingering attacks of malaria, was unable to offer his own. My father looked drawn; my mother had been crying. She was agitated to find me awake on the couch, but the woman explained that I wasn't feeling well. My mother removed her gloves and found my forehead burning and my chest covered in a red rash. Certain that I had yet another strain of measles, she hurried off to prepare cold wet cloths to cover my eyes. I can still feel the dampness of my bangs, the texture of my blanket, and the aura of escalating fever.

In the morning, my fever was so high that my mother called the doctor. I remember anxious stricken faces and wet sheets and the feeling that my feet did not touch the ground. Though no other cases had been reported in the Philadelphia area, I had contracted scarlet fever and was immediately placed under quarantine. The doctor said that afflicted children were typically kept at home for a couple weeks, but as we were in the middle of a polio epidemic, she advised several weeks of convalescence. The local health department tacked a large QUARANTINED sign on the door. My siblings were spirited off to relatives.

On that same afternoon Stephanie Holt died of uremia in the Abington Memorial Hospital. She was twelve years old. I would never again bask within her knowing presence, never be able to right my wrong. I would never be punished as no one suspected what I had done. Far worse than the prospect of hellfire I feared losing favor with God. Days after Stephanie died, I would inherit many of her belongings, given to me by her distraught mother. The comic books I coveted and the cigar box full of charms I had so admired, now too sick to acknowledge them but conscious enough to comprehend the terrible irony.

Continuing fevers melding with heavy doses of penicillin must have produced hallucinations. I felt myself lifted several inches from the mattress, my limbs lengthened, and my feet grew out of proportion. A nurse with the head of a red fox balancing a silver tray of syringes advanced slowly toward my bed. The syringes were filled with a thick penicillin that seemed to enter the bloodstream slowly. I was unable to get out of bed and unearth my great-grandfather's crumbling manual. But I secretly believed I would not find a remedy for what I was suffering, not merely a victim of scarlet fever but something much deeper, impossible to combat. Scarlet fever was my mystical illness, it crept into me just as life drained from Stephanie.

One thing I was certain of, I would prevail. I would be like Jo March, who drew from the fever of her imagination to tell stories. She lost her dear sister Beth to complications from scarlet fever and wrote a classic in her memory. Reading *Little Women,* I mourned Beth, I also knew I was not her. I would keep going, though I hadn't imagined that one day, like Jo March, I would pick up my pen to write. After ten days I was still weak, and my skin was peeling. Polio was epidemic and my mother, fearing complications of rheumatic fever, kept me home for several more weeks. With my mother and father working and my siblings away, I would lie alone with my books, propped up, the radio tuned to my father's classical station. Sometimes I would hear something that would fill me with a nameless emotion. One morning, I heard a voice so beautiful that I felt transported to another realm. I wrote down the name of the song, an aria from *Madama Butterfly,* and would listen attentively to the radio, hoping to hear it again.

Easter arrived late that year. My mother laid out a grey dress with a red ribbon. I was spindlier than ever and had lost some hair. The fastest runner in the neighborhood wobbly on her feet. My father took me outside, my first time since early February. He walked away and bade me come toward him, which I did with determined jerky movements. I could feel joy and relief radiating from Toddy and Linda as I took my first unsteady steps and kept on walking. Soon I would be racing through the high grass of the Patch with none able to outpace me.

Returning home from my first day back to school, I found all my belongings gone. My beloved tattered rabbit, my blue pajamas, all of Stephanie's charms and comics, including the very first issue of Superman, had all been placed in the basement furnace, transformed into antiseptic dust. Everything had been burned as a requirement from the Board of Health. I was devastated, yet my vague sense of the balances of justice helped to quell the sting of loss. A continuous sense of charity flowed through me, not from a heavenly source but the ghost of a girl in a nightgown propped up by a mountain of pillows on her sickbed. She had let me prattle on about my plans to see the world, the pagodas of Kyoto, the cathedrals of France, the pyramids, and the Taj Mahal. Stephanie, pale angel of atonement, never lived to see any of these places. I would see many such sites in my travels, at last forgiving myself for surviving.

I DID NOT want to grow up. I didn't aspire to be a member of the adult world, with its endless responsibilities. I wanted to be free to roam, to construct room by room the architecture of my own world. But the unstoppable mechanism of change was coming. I was most moved by the weed trees and would be saddened to find them felled. Still not quite dead, they oozed a milky substance from their slim branches. They were regarded as a nuisance, but they touched my lying heart. I lingered around the borders of the train tracks, where they still dominated. I had a growth spurt; I felt one with them as they grew quickly. You are my bamboo, I would whisper, the princesses of the train yard.

My mother depended on her youngest brother, Bobby. He was a good man, who never seemed like a grown-up as there was always something innocent about him. He was not bestowed with the best of luck but possessed an undeniable core of goodness. When another, more aggressive eviction notice arrived, my mother took things in her own hands and drove to South Jersey with Uncle Bobby, hoping to find an affordable home suitable for a family of five, a dog, and a cat. She had read of a small development called Woodbury Gardens and chose a plot for the least expensive choice of model homes. Uncle Bobby drove us to see the plot when my father was working. It was situated at the end of a road flanked by wetlands, winding into the perimeter of a massive pig farm. It felt private, with a long narrow sloping backyard. Across the way were several acres of Quaker land with an old black barn and a newer one with the words HOEDOWN HALL painted above the door. Beyond the field was a peach orchard. The house cost $9,999 and it took my parents thirty years to repay the high-interest loan, a fact that still breaks my heart.

On the weekends we drove out to observe the slow progress of the construction of our future home. My mother wanted to better our lives. But we kids believed we were just fine where we were. But our Patch was thinning out. I watched sadly as vacant lots were being cleared for future housing. A heavy dark atmosphere pervaded, and yet, out of the shade emerged an unexpected brightness, a new friend. Klara was plain, with grey eyes and light brown braids. I passed her house when I took an alternate route back home from school. One afternoon she beckoned me to come sit with her on the glider inside the screened porch. The motion made me feel sick to my stomach, so we planted our feet firmly to keep it still. Then she opened the book on her lap, filled with pictures of all kinds of exotic plants and herbs. She wanted to be a scientist, perhaps a botanist.

I could see inside the house but was not invited in. I promised to return and the next time I visited I brought an old heavy textbook that had belonged to my Uncle Bobby. It was filled with illustrations of single-celled animals, amphibians, planaria, the curves of shells and cross sections of crustaceans. She was enthralled with it. Her eagerness to devour contrasted with the incurious eyes of Stephanie. For the next few weeks, I visited her whenever I could slip away.

Klara lived with her uncle who always seemed worried and preoccupied, looking at his pocket watch, and then at the empty street through the screen door. He made us tea in heavy glasses from their former home in Bohemia. She showed me a small ruby bud vase etched with tiny white deer. I wondered if it had belonged to her mother but didn't ask. We didn't talk much; we communed, slowly moving through the pages of the same book. I was fond of the peace that descended upon us, the long silences, each undisturbed by the other. Sometimes a smile would turn into laughter, over nothing really. Once we laughed so much that her uncle appeared at the screen door, and for a moment the sun broke through, and he smiled as well. We took turns sweeping the porch and raking the early falling leaves.

One chilly afternoon I stopped to see Klara after school and saw that she had been crying. She told me they would soon be leaving. We held hands, sitting on the glider as we had always done. Returning home, I was caught in a sudden, torrential rain. I stepped in a massive puddle and my shoes filled with water and I caught a chill. My mother kept me home until I was better. It was only a few days, and as soon as I was well, I removed the heavy grey textbook from the bookcase to give it to Klara as a present, even if it meant being punished. Excited by the prospect, I raced to her house. The moment I approached the house I felt uneasy, the glider still, the screen ajar. I knew they were gone. I left the book outside and entered their house for the first time. I searched the rooms, each sparsely furnished, no trinkets, not the slightest human touch. On the floor of the smaller bedroom was Klara's book of botanical plants with several pages torn out. I imagined her on a path scattered with colored plates of flora and fauna, disembodied and sad.

The old houses, including Klara's and our condemned

compound were finally slated for full demolition. In memory, façades and empty spaces appear unaltered, where I occasionally revisit her room, mottled light streaming through chintz curtains, lingering upon the wood floor. The blur of a swing in vague motion. The abrupt disappearance of Klara affected me differently than the death of Stephanie. I was never able to share the mystery of Klara with anyone, she was my secret, and as time passed, I had to reassure myself that she truly existed.

Stephanie gave me a story, an unconscious moral lesson, but in the end, it was Klara who propelled me as a writer, even though I wasn't yet ready to write. The chasms of Klara provided an inaudible exercise; I would find myself pushing through membranes, mentally scrawling across the void. The imagined adventures of a Bohemian girl with thick braids, grey eyes, and thin square shoulders: Klara the scientist. Klara the fervent detective. Klara boarding a ship to explore the rain-forests of the Amazon. I never wrote these stories down; they live within the liminal threshold of my becoming.

THE FINAL EVICTION letter arrived. Everyone was leaving and much of our furniture was placed in storage. In the center of October, Hazel, one of the most intense hurricanes of 1954, swept over Philadelphia. My mother was terrified, ordering us to lie flat beneath the kitchen table for hours as gale force winds howled, and lightning struck the surrounding trees followed by a blackout. Huge fallen trees blocked the entrance to the Patch. My father spent the night in the dark climbing over dislodged rocks and wreckage in the heavy rain and high winds. In the morning, I went out with him to inspect the damage. A massive tree fell through the roof of the farthest building directly into an infant's room. My father joined the other men hoisting the massive limb above the crib. The infant trapped below was unharmed; everyone said it was a miracle. The juxtaposition of the destructive power of nature rivaled the ongoing demolition, and we excitedly climbed the rubble that no one bothered to clear as an unforgiving winter set in.

December 30, 1954, my birthday, was our last day at the Patch. I climbed up the stairs looking down at my feet. My oxfords were always a little big, stuffed with toilet paper in the toes, as I grew out of them so quickly. I took my first steps in the kitchen in Chicago shortly before my first birthday. When I learned to walk, I desired nothing more than to flee from my very pregnant mother. My young heart lamenting the passing of time, I revisited the places I loved with a kind of nostalgic urgency. The plundered poorhouse, the lanky weed trees, the abandoned home with its overrun yard. I tossed my last pennies upon the hallowed ground and watched them disappear in the snow. One day, I promised, I will tell about you.

The following morning, on New Year's Eve, my mother hurried us along as my uncle waited for us in the car. I lingered as I had yet to resolve a certain dilemma. The skater pin with 1952 emblazed at her feet remained beneath the floorboards. As I pulled on my coat I made my decision. I was eight years old; a new year was about to unfold. I did not retrieve my strange treasure, the pin, the plaster saint, and my telepathic toothbrush. I did not say goodbye. I simply left.

MY MOTHER HAD chosen our immediate destiny, trading one condemned compound for another. We had been one of the last families to leave the Patch, and now one of the only families inhabiting a building slated for demolition on East Bristol Street, in the Juanita district of northeast Philadelphia. A six-month holding pattern until our house in South Jersey was ready. It was the best my mother could do at the time. Though it was only four miles away we were never to see our beloved Patch again; Linda, Todd, and I were in a state of unconscious mourning.

We were surrounded with vacant structures. My memory of this area is a jaundiced abstract canvas, a sickly pale yellow with one red diagonal stripe, rows of attached brick houses, and a polluted sky. I was fixated on detective stories then, devouring Nancy Drew and Trixie Belden. The uneasy atmosphere of the surrounding streets suited my amateur detective's mind. We had no neighbors, except for two brothers camped out with their partially blind grandmother. The Docherty boys were unruly, aggressive, played Mumblety-peg with butcher knives instead of penknives, and killed rats with a hammer. I didn't fear them, but they were taller than me and I kept my distance.

Linda and I walked to Francis Hopkinson School, resembling a massive nineteenth-century asylum, only three blocks away. The short walk was a welcome change from the two-mile trek we had made to our country-style school in Germantown. January was mild, and I remember sun, no shadows, an urban de Chirico.

One morning Linda was sick and had to stay home in bed, so I headed to school at my own fast pace. Normally, I would accommodate her, as she did her best to keep up, smiling apologetically when she fell behind. Without the comforting presence of my sister our new schoolyard was a lonely place. No one was mean, I was simply invisible, certainly nobody's hero. I wore a plaid eye patch to strengthen my wandering eye; my string of illnesses had made its mark on my appearance and my brown plaid school bag inexplicably smelled of ants. I remember crossing the road, walking briskly and sliding in freshly laid tar. The latch on my lunch box broke and my new thermos hit the ground hard. Hurrying, I scooped it up and put it back but had to stop and remove a shoelace to tie around the lunch box to keep it shut. At lunch I sat alone and poured my warm cocoa into the red plastic cap, the smooth glass lining veined like a road map, a network of tiny cracks.

Local elections were drawing near and a candidate for town council visited the school. He brought an enormous sheet of cardboard covered with badges adorned with flowing ribbons like medals of honor. He offered them during recess. I deeply coveted one but was strictly forbidden to accept gifts from strangers. Every morning before we walked to school, my mother would say, Don't get into any stranger's car, don't take anything from a stranger. I stood alone by a wall. The young politician, perhaps reading my reticence as shyness, came over and asked if I wanted one of the remaining badges. I just hung my head and mumbled that I didn't want one. I dispiritedly joined my classmates, proudly sporting badges as we filed back to class. I thought of the medals of soldiers, runners, and great scientists like Madame Curie. It's okay, I said to myself, some-day I will do something special, and earn my own medals.

As spring approached, we sensed our mother's excitement and our father's absence, working overtime to help pay for our move in June. One evening, freshly bathed, hair combed, pajamas on, we begged our mother to show us the family pictures. Though much of our belongings were in storage, she kept the box of pictures with us for fear of losing them. I dragged a chair to the bedroom closet, reached up and grabbed the huge white box, but felt something moving and dropped it. My mother cried out as a flurry of rats scurried in all directions. Horrified she bent down and opened the lid. We gasped in chorus seeing nothing but shreds. All the precious mementos were gone. Baptismal certificates and fragile newspaper clippings: *Lindbergh Baby Kidnapped, Roosevelt Dead, War Is Over.* The first half of the twentieth century randomly captured through the lens of an old box camera. Daddy Frank on a donkey. Young Marguerite holding my mother. My father in his uniform. Unidentified army buddies. My mother in a nightclub with upswept hair. Aunt Gloria in her tap shoes. Bambi as a puppy. The three of us armed with hot dogs on a stick, smiling through the smoke of Aunt Dot's barbecue. Every irreplaceable photograph returned to the bygone, shred-ded for nest material, like strands of chaw tobacco and black confetti. All the pictures that had excited our eager eyes and drew out our inquisitive minds. We were all heartsick. My mother cried for days. It occurred to me later the sole surviving remnant of the past belonged to me, the ghost of my father breaking through a ribbon in an old tin frame.

# The Gardens

M Y FATHER LIVED in his own world; he left the new world to my mother. We departed the dismal apartment on East Bristol Street, just days before it was bulldozed, for our ranch house in the middle of nowhere. It was our twelfth move since I was born, all carefully documented in my baby book. At first, I resented moving to a rural area, missing the traces of urban debris, the trees of heaven dominating vacant lots and the mournful sounds of passing trains. The change from an apartment to a house was disconcerting. Our voices echoed in the empty rooms. There were two bedrooms and each of us had our own twin bed. My mother slept on the big green pull-out couch, waiting for my father to come home from the night shift.

It was a small development, struggling lower-middle-class families of soldiers, grateful to have their first home. The yards were bare, dry, and unappealing. But across the road peach blossoms covered the ground like a battlefield in Shiloh. At night long black snakes slithered from the swampy areas, swarms of mosquitoes and gnats, butterflies in abundance, long pale green luna moths, muskrats, barn owls, and, in our yard, an occasional wild pig. The appearance of such a hairy behemoth prompted a favorite family joke. My mother was hanging laundry in the backyard when she burst through the kitchen door.

—Grant, she cried breathlessly, there's a boar in the yard!

—Then don't talk to him, he said, not looking up from his newspaper.

She pretended to be annoyed but soon we were all laughing. We congregated in the kitchen on Sundays, the one morning due to our parents' work schedules that we could all be together.

My mother was overjoyed to have a real home with an eat-in kitchen where her new friends could drink coffee, smoke cigarettes, and share their troubles. My father was a gifted calligrapher; he rendered *A friend knocks before he enters, not after he leaves* above the back door. None of us fully understood the meaning. He instructed us to reason it out for ourselves.

My father couldn't afford a car. He walked two miles in all weather to catch a bus to Philadelphia, still working the night shift at Honeywell. My mother got a job at a lunch counter at a fair-sized pharmacy in an early strip mall. Before too long, she pretty much ran it. We made our own dinner, usually fish sticks, Dinty Moore stew, or grilled cheese, whatever we could make ourselves. Without supervision, we lived mostly outdoors and past twilight, we'd huddle together beneath the blackness of the country night animated with bright patterns of mythical beings.

Thomas's Field was different from the Patch, but rampant with its own magic. The Thomas family were Quakers and had

owned the thirteen-acre field for generations, most likely former Lenape land. They seldom spoke to us but were kind and
didn't seem to mind us playing on their property. Farmer Baker
across the way was extremely unfriendly. When his peaches fell
to the ground, we'd shimmy through the high grass and gather
them for my mother to make pie. He patrolled the area with a
shotgun filled with salt rock, which more than once found its
mark. There was an outhouse by the road that I sometimes
used, as our small bathroom was often occupied. I didn't mind
it, nor the ants crawling across my shoes. It was all captivating,
sleeping in the grass, pissing in a hole, a peanut butter sandwich
wrapped in a bandana, lunch in the woods. Wrestling with an
independent streak I still committed my child crimes, exploring forbidden territory, displaying indifference to my mother's
sufferings, removing a coin from my sleeping father's trousers.
An endless gallery of trespasses.

Television provided new sources of inspiration. Buster
Crabbe, who we had venerated in the role of Flash Gordon,
was back as Captain Gallant of the Foreign Legion, hero of the
galaxy and now the desert. With red rags tied around our
heads, Toddy and I would dramatically crawl as if lost in the
desert and Linda would rescue us with a water bottle. We
enacted our dehydration dramas at the field's edge that merged
with the off-limits, and somewhat treacherous, gravel pit,
where teenage boys congregated and smoked cigarettes.

The Davy Crockett series starring Fess Parker and Buddy
Ebsen had captured young American hearts and we were no
exception. We'd play in the woods, searching for bears and
wildcats. I found a toy rifle that looked like an old Winchester

at a church bazaar, a single metal barrel with a wood handle. I carved Old Betsy on it like Davy did. One Sunday, aiming at an invisible target in the yard, my father appeared behind me, enraged. He snatched the rifle from my hand, snapped it in half, and threw it on the ground, forbidding the three of us to ever point a gun, even a toy, at any living thing.

We had never seen him like that. My mother later told us he most likely was thinking of the war. He had been shipped to Australia, New Guinea, and then the Philippines to fight the Japanese. Many of his men died of friendly fire, stumbling fearfully through sniper and snake infested jungles, drenched in fever. My father still suffered cluster migraines from malaria. He was not wounded, but he came back broken and brokenhearted; the atomic bombs dropped on Hiroshima and Nagasaki forever paled his patriotism. Nothing could justify so much death and destruction in a single moment, not even in retaliation. It remained one of his greatest sorrows, a uniquely American shame.

It was the summer before fourth grade. The three of us shifted the colors of our adventures. We no longer emulated others nor mentally boarded our small golden ship sailing the Milky Way. Instead, we were just ourselves and trekked the surrounding wetlands captivated by strange blooms, swamp pinks and meadow rue, avoiding skunk cabbage and looking out for paper wasps and stinging yellow jackets. We discovered cattails in the marshes that we lit, pretending we were smoking. The other end of the development had a sprawling wood, dominated by a massive mound of tons of red earth that we christened Red Clay Mountain; we named everything, and the names remain. Up the way was the armory, a big brick building with a tank on the grounds, more adornment than armament, where once a month there were teenage dances.

On Sunday nights there were square dances at Hoedown Hall. The grown-ups reeled and waltzed, and we ran through the field chasing lightning bugs, with the sounds of stomping and fiddles drifting in the air. Unable to sleep I would slip out and look across at the thorny brambles entwining high scrub bushes just across the road. They seemed to shiver in the moonlight and at some point, I became certain that it was the dwelling place of God. These were my alone thoughts, ones that I could not translate into the theater of our play. There was something about the field that mystified, even troubled me. It seemed to possess an energy of its own accompanied

with a barely perceptible dissonant music, long after the fiddlers had departed.

In early mornings I would often explore the woods alone with Bambi. She was meek, never ran off and needed no leash. We'd trace the movements of tadpoles in Rainbow Creek, silently track an elusive red fox, or lie together in the dewy field beneath the wide empty sky. I came to appreciate our new home and the surrounding area, especially Thomas's Field. There were spirits everywhere, one could sense them, air crackling the clouds haloed in rose-colored light. And so, we went from the Patch, where bits of nature were given wild, to the Gardens, where my mother planted flowers, and my father tended hedges that were trimmed so perfectly and grew so high they seemed worthy of a sketch in *Alice's Adventures in Wonderland.* There was mystery here, not so much in the people, but in the land itself, in the barns, the outhouse, surrounding wetlands, the red earth containing the clay of being. I felt it calling to me, inviting me to experience a frequency I had not yet known. I was consumed with a sense that each of us knows everything, possessing our own lock and the key to turn it. I wondered what I would find, what my contribution might be, and what I might add to the infinite pool above.

MY MOTHER WAS very close to Daddy Frank and forgiving toward her young stepmother who had tried to manipulate her in keeping me for herself. When he died unexpectedly of heart failure she was inconsolable. I woke in the middle of the night to the sound of breaking glass and found her sobbing before the remains of my piggy bank, counting out the pathetic mound of coins she needed to get a bus to Chattanooga for his funeral. Months later she remained uncharacteristically melancholy, until Jehovah's Witnesses came to our door and offered her hope that she might reunite with her beloved parents in a new post-apocalyptic system.

She swiftly became a devoted Witness and eventually took me to all the meetings. Having had strong scriptural training I adapted quickly, though at times found being in a religion somewhat confining. My father read and analyzed the Bible regularly but rejected organized religion; I felt that his method of study suited me better. My mother emotionally embraced her faith but was unable to fully commit and gradually drifted away. She pinned her faith on me to keep a strong relationship with the Witnesses, which I did, including having to sacrifice Saturday morning cartoon shows to go door to door preaching the good news. In the 1950s Jehovah's Witnesses were greatly misunderstood and persecuted. Buckets of urine and excrement were often thrown on us when hostile people opened their doors on a Saturday afternoon. It was this treatment that most drew me to them, as my penchant for siding with the downtrodden or those discriminated against had been well nourished by both of my parents.

When I started fourth grade at my new school, I wore a middy blouse and my hair in a ponytail. I was not the sickly weird one as I had been in Philadelphia. I was like everyone else, only taller and skinnier, but no one seemed to care. It was soon apparent that I was no longer the fastest runner, and I reasoned that I would have to discover something new that would make me special. Being a Witness, I did not salute the flag in the morning, though I did recite the Lord's Prayer. I didn't mind any ridicule for not saluting the flag, for at eight I was beginning to feel conflicted about pledging my allegiance completely. I wanted to know about everything: the layers of heaven, possible other worlds, the inside of rocks, what lay between the pages of unattainable books, what people really thought but didn't say, what invisible force kept us in line, what held us back and what propelled us forward. While everyone slept, such thoughts spinning, I felt encased in a floating globule. If only I could poke through it with my finger, it might dissolve, water would rise to an opening in the ceiling, and I'd be carried away.

I had successfully vanquished TB, scarlet fever, measles, mumps, and chicken pox but then I was struck with the A (H2N2) virus during the Asian flu pandemic. I felt overpowered from every front. Once again, I was quarantined, my siblings whisked away to a neighbor. This virus possessed the multiple swords of a vindictive deity. I suffered high fever, nausea, and crippling body pain; I could only lie and pray for oblivion. In the distance I could hear our pediatrician speaking to my weeping mother. I remember her saying, "I don't know if she will make it, Beverly." I wanted to dispute her but could not speak. I could hear them as if they were far away, yet only standing by my bed. My mind tried to reach out, tell them I would make it, but I couldn't move or open my eyes.

My memories of this illness are minimal, more like bits of deteriorating film—sips of water, ice packs, my mother's desperation, the vise cluster of migraines encasing my small skull. I remember ceasing to care. On the kitchen shelf was a mason jar filled with tip money for groceries and emergencies. Every penny accounted for. I discerned the sound of cascading coins; my mother slipped out with the money from the jar. Half conscious, I felt something weighty placed on my chest. I was too weak to open my eyes but felt the object with my hand. It was a box set containing a recording of *Madama Butterfly,* with the libretto in English and Italian. I could not even respond. She said I could listen to it anytime I wanted, but not until I was well. Then she reached for it, but I didn't want to let it go and she let me hold it awhile longer.

In the days and nights that followed, the wish to escape my body was only surpassed by a yearning to listen to the music of Puccini. There was no amount of penicillin or prayer more effective than my mother's loving proviso. She placed the box atop the dresser so I could see it. I would drift in and out, yet another pounding migraine, but could also feel myself getting stronger, healing cells multiplying. I drank water, ate my Jell-O and slept. The sight of the box with a delicate sketch of Butterfly in her headdress and kimono spurred me on.

When I recovered, I was finally able to hear the aria *Un bel di Vedremo,* once again transported by a voice that seemed a celestial messenger. There were three discs inside, each one with a winged cherub on the Angel label. I labored over the difficult libretto, but in truth I didn't need to know the words of the aria.

My mother had emptied the tip jar, no doubt sacrificing much. I remember all of this. My fiery desire to hear the music of Puccini coupled with my mother's deep understanding of how she could reach me through the barriers of a relentlessly burning fever. The wedding of art and sacrifice. That is how I returned to the world.

My tenth birthday was approaching. What I wanted most in life was a bicycle, so I could travel faster and go off on my own, but my parents could never afford one. This was different from my hunger for books or my fascination with talismanic objects. It was a visceral need to be free. When the day arrived so soon after Christmas, it was uneventful, and I was disappointed in the family's apparent disinterest. In the evening, my father asked me to help install the glass shower door my mother had been saving for. I could hardly disguise my feelings, sullen and slow moving. He ignored my reluctance and asked me to help him dislodge it from the huge box. He would push one end, and I would reach in and pull from the other. Why me, I was thinking, as I reached inside the massive cardboard box. To my astonishment I extracted a twenty-one-inch blue Schwinn with foot brakes. I could hardly speak as my father assembled the handlebars and kickstand, and the next morning I went flying down the hill as soon as I impatiently finished breakfast. A few days later I noticed my mother had replaced our old plastic shower curtain with yet another, trading her vision of glass doors for my own heart's desire.

I was told by my father not to race on my bicycle, but I loved speed. I was racing down a steep hill, when a massive swarm of gnats rushed toward me. Completely enveloped, I panicked, and trying to brake, my right foot got caught in the bicycle chain and I crashed. Most likely I fractured a bone in my foot as a painful bump appeared, though I was still able to hobble back up the hill with my bike. Use your head, my father would repeatedly say. I didn't want my father to know that I hadn't, so I asked my brother to tape up my foot, and though I limped about, no one seemed to notice.

Later I tried to map what I had done wrong. I let fear take over and lost focus on the task at hand. I should've stayed calm, even as the gnats swirled about me into my eyes and up my nose. They were not harmful, more a nuisance, and I should've stayed measured and rode through it. I was not the kind of kid that cowered during a heavy storm. I often slipped outside unnoticed to watch the lightning; I was disappointed that I had been so rattled so easily.

My father often read us poems aloud, especially verses of counsel. He sat us down and read us Kipling's poem *If*. The first lines spoke to me immediately, *If you can keep your head when all about you / Are losing theirs,* a mantra I much preferred over my father's personal commandment of *Use your head*. I considered the champions in fairy tales, burdened with multiple challenges, they prevailed by keeping a clear head, avoiding foretold temptations and distractions. I told myself that one cannot fail due to irrational fear. One must face danger squarely but with respect and cunning. My foot eventually healed, though there was a small spur of a bone protruding under my skin, reminding me of my failing. Keep your head, I would tell myself; adversity is but a swarm of gnats.

My mother unexpectedly became pregnant again. Linda was the most excited about the prospect of a new sibling. In early August 1957, Kimberly was born. She was a small chubby happy little thing who looked exactly like my mother. When my mother was ready to return to work, she took the night shift entrusting Kimberly's care to the three of us. She had a sunny personality but was also severely asthmatic. When she was rushed to the hospital, the doctor ordered all allergens in our home removed, an entire cleansing of our house, our familial disorder. The first to go was the big green brocade couch, with its protruding rusted springs and suspected mites. It was retired and ceremoniously put outside with the trash. The three of us sat on it together, facing the road, reminiscing, then falling silent. We knew it was necessary, a monumental touchstone of a time we could sense ending, cracks in the protective shell of childhood. Not necessarily innocence, but the aura and collective spirit created by the three of us. There was a new child. New worries and new responsibilities. My childhood as I knew it was ending. I knew it was true yet prayed a new prayer. Let me stay ten, with my dog, my books, and my bicycle.

The beginning of a game. Children in love with everything. Spinning simultaneously, falling dizzily in one another's arms. A blur of joy that was slowly dissipating. We were playing rough, wrestling around in the backyard. It was a hot summer day. My mother called me in the house and told me to put a shirt on. I protested, as it was too hot, and Toddy wasn't wearing a shirt. My mother said I had to wear one as I was becoming a young lady. This sudden information shocked and repelled me. I imagined I could sidestep change, physical evolution. I was only interested in the evolving mind, in freedom. I felt stunned and sickened, but I could not fight my mother. I didn't want to be a boy any more than a young lady. I just wanted to be myself. I put on my shirt and went to the woods alone and read *Peter Pan*. Neverland seemed another kind of religion, offering a child's paradise where one never had to grow up.

I loved my family, yet I felt suffocated. Only my devotion to my siblings kept me from running away. Even so, where would I go? Spindly thing without a dime and with a chronic cough. And so, though visible to all, I would sometimes disappear. I sat stirring up the tadpoles with a stick. I did not take my shirt off, as I could feel as always, even from afar, my mother watching. I had the sense of an invisible but palpable shift. No words, just a feeling. I did not want to choose between Peter the boy or Wendy the girl. It was better to contain both, dwell within a hut in a protected forest, surrounded by waving ferns, marshes, and moths the color of the moon.

Kimberly had another serious asthma attack and once again was taken to the hospital. This time we had to face the sacrifice of our beloved pets. My mother's cat, Mittens, and our faithful Bambi. This was no one's fault, but we were all brokenhearted. My mother promised Bambi to a family I knew from school; the girl reminded me of Suzanne, taunting me with the fact that soon my dog would be hers. I thought of running away with Bambi, bitterly thinking if I couldn't have her no one else should.

On Sunday morning I rose early and took Bambi to Red Clay Mountain. We sat by Rainbow Creek and I told her everything that would transpire. She looked in my eyes and I truly believed she understood. Then we went to Thomas's Field. A beautiful Indian summer day. We lay in the grass, looking up at the clouds together. She rested her deerlike face on my lap and we fell asleep. When I awoke, the position of the sun had changed. I had no idea what time it was and raced across the field home. Bambi ran off before me, which was unlike her as she always stayed by my side. I called out to her to wait, and she stopped in the middle of the road. Reaching the edge of the field I called out to her again. She just stood looking at me, our eyes locked for what seemed to be several moments, but most likely fleeting seconds. Out of nowhere a speeding fire truck turned the bend and struck her right before my eyes. The driver braked and approached us. I reached for her and cried out.

My father came running, trailed by my siblings. He gathered her up and wrapped her in a soft blanket and we buried her at the side of the house. Several hours later the other family pulled up to collect her, and my father explained that Bambi had died. Not a word of reproach was said. There was a quiet sense of mourning. For years I was to replay that scene over and over, suspecting that I was subconsciously complicit in the death of Bambi. It was Linda, the empathetic one, who found a way to render me guiltless. Bambi didn't want to leave us, she said. She did it herself.

Fall was approaching; there wasn't a single cloud but rolling thunder could be heard in the distance and sudden flashes of blue-sky lightning streaked the sky. Out of nowhere a bolt struck, setting fire to the old black barn. It was a cause of great excitement; Toddy darted across the road to join the fast-gathering onlookers, but I had to stay behind with Kimberly. Holding her in my arms, I watched with a heavy heart from our driveway as the ramshackle barn surrendered to the flames. I had loved that old barn, nothing inside but owls, bats, massive spiderwebs, and broken tools, barely visible save for thin shafts of dusty light. I resented that I could not join them, but looking at Kimberly, her little moon face smiling at me pleasantly, I felt a sense of peace. Later Toddy described the scene, a mass exodus of critters, screaming bats, and then a creaking gasp as it toppled over, like the crushed top hat of Harpo Marx.

IT WAS 1959, the year of Mandrake the Magician, the year of uncertain, explosive magic. Before I learned to read, I would stare at the Sunday comics, completely mesmerized by Mandrake with his blue-black cape that gave the impression it had been cut from the night. I wondered if it had dropped from the sky onto his shoulders. I'd imagine having something transmutable like Mandrake's cloak or the banner and sword of Joan of Arc. I had not yet discerned that the imagination, the talisman of thought, was far greater than a traveling carpet or a cloak of invisibility. But I did recognize the difference between objects of virtue and mere treasure, and as in all great tales of valor, one must do something worthy with such powers.

When I saw *Lost Horizon,* the film adapted from the book by James Hilton, I was captivated by the kingdom of Shangri-La, where no one ever ages. I found the book in a library; inside was a yellowed newspaper clipping with an interview with the author who explained he was inspired by ancient Tibetan scriptures. This led to a new preoccupation; I was drawn to Tibetan culture, ecstatic by the thought of hidden civilizations. I pictured monks guarding secret knowledge and practicing the mystery of flight. It gave me hope that angels did not die with the sealing of the Scriptures, they had simply repositioned themselves on the roof of the world, where monks prayed for the earth ceaselessly, even as others destroyed it.

Our sixth-grade teacher assigned us to compile a scrapbook for social studies. We were asked to choose a country, cutting and pasting newspaper articles, reporting on it weekly. Most everyone chose European countries, but I chose Tibet to the ridicule of my classmates and the frustration of my teacher. She wasn't even sure that Tibet was a real country, but when I pointed it out on the globe flanked by India, Nepal, and China, she reluctantly let me keep it.

*Lost Horizon* led me to Tibet that led me to Buddhism and an awareness of the interconnectedness of all things. Although this seemed beautiful it nonetheless troubled me. It was as if the universe was a hologram I could observe and even touch and yet did not feel part of. Perhaps I lacked the empathy to identify with the entire universe. I was too immersed in my own world. Seeing *The Incredible Shrinking Man* with my siblings I was horrified by the ending, the shrinking man dematerializing. I couldn't help resisting the concept of dissipation, surrendering to the cosmos, even to God. What I wished for was a path that contained everything, and that each of us could extract through our imagination an individually experienced connectiveness with the past, present, and future.

Though I knew it was wrong, I prayed for something to happen in Tibet, some news I could spotlight. Each week during social studies hour while my classmates filled their scrapbooks, mine remained empty. My exasperated teacher implored me to change countries, but I was too stubborn, too loyal, and I held my ground, doubling my prayer energy at bedtime.

On March 11, 1959, Tibetan rebels attacked Chinese officials, and the Chinese government launched an offense against Tibet, capturing Lhasa. The fourteenth Dalai Lama, then twenty-three, fled on foot. Tibet, my seemingly forgotten country, was front page news. My father collected articles from the various papers his co-workers were reading. Everything one could hope for to enliven a social studies report, photographs, maps, and the continuing drama of the escape of the missing Dalai Lama. All were astounded, as if I had a special relationship with the future. Awarded the highest grade, my report was displayed in a glass case, a bittersweet school victory. My once secret country now belonged to the world stage. I felt my prayers, delivered with such adolescent fervor, had disrupted the ecosystem of fate. I had made a wish that only benefited myself and was bitten on the heel by a malevolent genie.

I followed the path of the young Dalai Lama in my mind, praying for his safety as he went by foot through treacherous terrain, from Lhasa through the Himalayas to India. Toward the end of April there was a portrait of the young Dalai Lama wearing his signature glasses on the cover of *Time* magazine. My mother brought it home for me. The Dalai Lama had safely reached the village of Tawang, just across the Indian border. Some believed he had been protected from Communist planes by mist and low clouds, conjured up by the prayers of Buddhist holy men. I had no doubt that their prayers had the power to invoke the protective clouds. But in fully believing in theirs I was obliged to consider the possible destructive power of mine.

I hopped on my bike fraught with conflicted emotions and flew down to the end of the hill to a prohibited fenced-in area, infested by snakes, mosquitoes, and quick mud. Unspoiled wetlands, where the call of strange birds led to a place not yet corrupted by the outside world. I laid my bike down, found a rend in the wire fence, slipped in, and tramped through the marsh. I squatted in the high grass; I was certain I was never going to be good. As I rose my rebel hump broke its child husk and sprouted the wiry bristles of a young boar.

# Illuminations

Art is the highest form of hope.

GERHARD RICHTER

I DON'T KNOW WHAT possessed my father to take us to a museum. Our sole family visit to the Philadelphia Museum of Art was a revelation. I discovered art. Not the idea of art, nor a picture in a magazine, but art in person. We had never been to a museum or a gallery, we had never been to the movies or a restaurant together. There was no money to do anything save to picnic in the summer together. Perhaps it was a discount family day, or simply because my father was enamored of Salvador Dalí, and the museum was hosting the exhibit Persistence of Memory. While my father admired the draftsmanship and surreal imagination of Dalí, I slipped away to look at things on my own. The life-sized canvases of Sargent were beautiful, in a Modigliani I recognized my own lanky frame. Then I entered an entire hall devoted to Picasso, that in memory lengthens and curves, evolving from a melancholy circus of the blue and rose harlequins to early Cubism.

My father set out looking for me and found me staring at a large Cubist painting. He wasn't impressed at all by Picasso, found Dalí superior as a draftsman with a more complex vision. I was smitten with Picasso and for the first time I realized my father and I had strong conflicting ideas, and I had no qualms about defending my point of view. I now felt I had superlative allies, who would one day lead me to a whole new world. I obediently followed my father out of the museum but held fast to an invisible transformation; I had fallen for art.

HIS NAME WAS Johnny Stahl. He lived down the hill to the first right. He shot rabbits and squirrels in the woods for food. My sister went to school with his sister. I don't remember him having a mother; I was wary of his father, a slim unsmiling man with silent darting glimpses. Johnny was quiet, confident. He gave me his brown boot lace for my skate key. It was my first gift from a boy; more gesture than gift, a beau geste.

I would park my bike and shyly approach the door and see if he was home. In the back, on the clothesline, rabbit skins were drying. I noticed a shotgun propped up by the door. Johnny seemed to stand apart. He was soft-spoken and kept to himself. He tied a raccoon tail on the handlebar of my bike, promising another. He didn't say much but when he did it always seemed the right thing. He had longish blond hair that fell in his eyes, like a young James Dean. We were unconscious versions of the brooding Cal and high spirited Abra in *East of Eden*. Our conversations remain in the sphere of time, not time lost, but time suspended.

There was a skating rink around a mile up the road, past the pig farm, and verging to the right. Johnny asked me to go skating with him on a Saturday. We walked there together; I remember a light breeze and how happy I was. A boy I liked, the benevolence of nature, and a shared sense of freedom. It cost 50 cents admission and another 25 cents to rent the skates. There were rows of them, white leather with wooden wheels. I can see him bending over to tie my white laces, and after several turns around the rink, he took my hand in his and we skated as if nothing in the world existed but this moment of mutual acceptance.

I relived that moment before falling asleep. I now had someone to share a blossoming interior world. But then there was silence. After a few days I impulsively got on my bike to seek him out. As I approached the house, I saw his father motioning for Johnny and his sister to hurry. They had an old paneled station wagon packed with their things, fishing poles and shotguns strapped atop a rack. His father was impatient. I braked my bike and watched Johnny get in the car with his head down. His father reversed slowly out of the driveway. Johnny pressed his open palm against the window. His face told me everything, including goodbye. That was our last moment. I was unable to reach the window of the car to press my own hand against the glass. The sun was in my eyes, and the station wagon pulled away and, with it, a young girl's dream.

I lay in the high grass of Thomas's Field looking up at an empty sky. There was life all around, yet I felt strangely unmoved. I could feel myself changing, things once dear to me receding, giving way to new concerns, new ways of seeing. I rode my bike past the street where Johnny had lived, the yard now overgrown and the house empty. I imagined the conversations we might have had. Now I had them with myself. *Question everything* was my mantra, certainly influenced by my father who always saw several sides of any argument. His questions were different from mine, but he magnified my penchant for questioning, offering a kind of permission, sometimes getting me into trouble.

Increasingly moody, I sat in Bible study plagued with disquieting thoughts, forming opinions about interpretations of Scriptures. I listened intently to an Elder describing the Apocalypse and the creation of a New World, and was overcome with jarring images of museums, sculpture, great architecture, to say nothing of Picasso's paintings, in flames. These thoughts churned in my conscience, burrowing a small hole, interrupting my sleep. I fretted over the aesthetics of the post Apocalypse, the décor of Christ's Kingdom. What will happen to art? This question meant everything to me, even as it was scoffed at. I was shaken when a respected man from the Congregation dismissively waved me away.

Days later I spoke to another Elder voicing my concerns. Perhaps I was too confrontational, for I was swiftly admonished. At that time questioning the high-ranking Elders in our Congregation was unacceptable. I was told that there was no place for art in Christ's Kingdom, and I was counseled to consider what I truly believed in. But I knew what I believed in. I believed in the Creator, the many tongues of nature, the moral lessons of fairy tales, the language of trees, and the clay of the Earth. I believed in the woolgatherers, soul-catchers, and monks who could leave their physical body and travel. I labored to form an equation that would include all things. God the infinite realm, Jesus the human bridge and the artist the material mouthpiece.

In the night I searched for a solution; the atmosphere seemed to contain a sense of ancestral messaging. I considered those way back in time gazing at skies and forming constellations, pictures generated by human imagination. Perhaps those who had the eyes to see pictures were some of our first artists. As a Jehovah's Witness I had placed my faith in the New System, but I wondered if there were many systems. Once it was believed that there was only one planet, one solar system, but in truth we discovered that there are many. It seemed to me being an artist was also a sacred profession, requiring great sacrifice. I spent many sleepless nights before making the decision to cease my Bible studies and not return to the Kingdom Hall. At the same time, I was more than grateful for the intense scriptural education I had received. I cast off my religion, not without escaping a bitter sorrow, yet also accompanied by a feeling of liberation. I had chosen my own path, gave my evolving self to art, and decided to prepare myself for the life of an artist pledging to be steadfast no matter the consequences.

Having freed myself from the rubrics of religion, I could think in any way I wanted. The braid of the mind seemed to have many strands winding around each other, containing everything. All of history, all of knowledge, waiting to reveal itself, if only one could crack the code. The face of Jesus, the Ark of the Covenant, God's telephone number, areas of the undiscovered universe, and the continuing adventures of fictional characters. We are born with a mind, open to everything, no fear, no known boundaries, but with each new rule, restriction the mind divides. We learn to live as in the age of reason, in relation to the world, to social order, balancing a compliance between imagination and the respirable kingdom. I believed wisdom and sacred mysteries were contained in a secret language found in my books, written by those who surely possessed even a few letters of an ancient alphabet. I was drawn to books before I could read a single word, intuiting wondrous things. Although I had read many books it hadn't yet occurred to me to write the endless stream of ideas flowing through my head. It seemed a natural part of being a reader; books were written by others. I began to write, but nothing successfully expressed a bright interior world. I had not found my voice.

One day I chanced upon *The Selfish Giant* by Oscar Wilde, strangely listed in *Children's Digest* as a fairy tale. It was not like any other I had read. I had the same shock of aesthetic recognition that I had experienced with the photographs in *Vogue,* the poems by Yeats, and the paintings of Picasso. I read it over and over, trying to garner his uniqueness. And then it struck me: Everything was a potential poem. The stoic prayers of the mantis, the knowing eyes of my dog, the pen scratching. The white snake stirred, and the invisible lines of the rebel hump flickered then shimmered like the coat of many colors.

My father rose from a perfect dive like a mythological god with bits of red cedar clinging to the hairs of his chest. He was a marvelous swimmer, graceful and athletic. This was our yearly family outing. In lieu of camp, many of the poorer neighborhood kids went to Baptist Bible school in summer.

Linda and I recited Scriptures then were herded onto buses with farm workers. We picked and ate blueberries for hours in the dizzying sun and took breaks to drink water from a hose. I moved slowly, resenting the task, amazed at the speed of the workers who could fill a bushel basket faster than I could fill a pint. At the end of the day, we were paid. The first time I made less than a dollar. I thought we were paid by the hour, not by the basket, and probably ate more than I picked.

At the closing of Bible school, our families were gifted with a free day at Centerton Lake. We roasted hot dogs and marsh-mallows. Our parents sat around talking, not of the war, but of the present, everyone struggling to get by. Their cheery gossip and laughter mingling with the splashing of the divers. Linda and I sat at the edge of the lake, we had been kept out of water during the polio epidemic, and neither of us learned to swim. It didn't bother me as I hated being submerged. We were happy we could give our family this day merely by slugging through Baptist Bible school. Linda and I rose and followed the music wafting from the pavilion jukebox and danced.

We all loved to dance, especially to the latest R&B and rock and roll songs that articulated swiftly forming adolescent long-ings. The year 1961 opened with the Shirelles singing *Will You Love Me Tomorrow,* one of the most beautiful and controversial songs of its time. It was banned by the Catholic Church yet reached number one on the charts, the first by a black female group. It was a time of great R&B songs expressing a full range of teenage concerns. Songs to dance to, cry to, or act out in front of the mirror. Music was our salvation, expressing the inex-pressible. We were a part of its evolution, the radio our lifeline.

With summer Bible school ending, the armory dances became a weekly thing. Two hours of babysitting would pay for entrance and a soda. The girls took forever to get ready, often undergoing impressive transformations. I had no interest in wearing a makeup mask, teasing and spraying my hair, being coy or playing games, which possibly made me less interesting to the boys. But I liked going to the armory dances; a few hours of spinning records, boys on one side, girls huddled together on the other, mostly girls dancing with girls. Dancing was a South Jersey pride. We were the best dancers, and I was pretty good, not the best, but not bad. At some point the boys from South Philadelphia started coming. Most of them wore leather jackets, but one of them, the quiet one, stood apart from the rest. He wore an overcoat, stood by the wall, just observing. Not an official leader, but definitely one who could not be led. His name was Butchy Magic, the face of my early teenage fantasies.

He attended the dances intermittently and I lived for these few hours of being in his proximity. I thought of him so much I felt he could see through me, that he must have known my heart. One summer evening, inspired by Li'l Abner, I gathered all my courage, contrived my own Sadie Hawkins Day, and asked him to dance. Sorry I don't dance, was all he said. I smiled and walked away, perhaps a bit embarrassed, but not disheartened. I danced by myself anyway, then sensing a general disquiet I decided to go outside, catch some air. I approached the door just as a skirmish broke out. I turned at the same moment someone threw a leather jacket and hit a hornet's nest in a low rafter right above me. The nest fell at my feet and the agitated hornets flew excitedly around me. The succession of events happened quickly; I was stung multiple times. I was so shocked I just stood there. Kids were yelling and the boys from Philly made a mass exit. I stood frozen, as they stampeded past me, a hornet fixed in my neck. Suddenly he was there, in front of me, looking straight in my eyes, as if commanding me to stay still. Holding my gaze, he slowly pulled the hornet and stinger out of my neck and placed it in his handkerchief, then departed not saying a word.

This is what the writer craves, in a café in the earliest hours, in an empty drawing room of a hotel, or scrawling in a note-book in the pew of a silent cathedral. A sudden shaft of bright-ness containing the vibration of a particular moment. Johnny Stahl tying my bootlace. Butchy Magic's fingers extracting the stinger. The unsullied memory of unpremeditated gestures of kindness. These are the bread of angels. The pen drops, I touch phantom wounds. The boys from Philly never returned. By the time I was fifteen the face of another pervaded my furtive fantasies. The angels served a new portion; I discovered Arthur Rimbaud.

On Saturday mornings I modeled at the Philadelphia Academy in exchange for drawing lessons. There was a 99-cent bookstall across from the bus station. I inspected it as usual and was drawn to the face of the young poet on the cover of *Illuminations*. Within a moment's reading I was as beguiled by his words as his insolent beauty. Not having a dollar, nor willing to part with it, I slid *Illuminations* in my pocket, a crime I did not regret. Although his work was somewhat impenetrable it offered a new poetic language. I searched the library for something of him and found the words that called to me, would call forth from me, fixed and ephemeral, *A Season in Hell,* my furious guidebook.

*A Season in Hell* is as much ignoble confession as poetry, Rimbaud concedes his seemingly supernatural power over language while displaying a vehement self-loathing. *You'll always be a hyena,* he writes, tearing himself in two, wrestling with the civil war of his personality. I recognized a relatable duality, the demonic hand in hand with the charitable. I was struck that he was barely nineteen, his suffering sealed within the pages of a book. I wanted to believe that his confession released him from his turmoil, and I sought to follow him down his shattering spiritual path.

Then, on my sixteenth birthday, my mother gave me a copy of *The Fabulous Life of Diego Rivera.* I had never read the biography of an artist and its effect on me was also profound, struck by arrows, though hardly poisonous. I followed his worldly adventures and his many phases, what he learned and discarded from Picasso, his engagement with political turmoil, and the heritage and personality of his native country. I was intrigued by images of the influential women in his life, the strong masculine face of Guadalupe Marín and the revolutionary artist Frida Kahlo. The book was a testament to the sacrifice, labor, and visionary integrity of the artist, that I longed to embrace as my own.

My mother had no idea how I would respond to such a book, nor other wondrous gifts she innocently gave me. She did her best to rein me in and yet unwittingly provided me with the handbooks of flight. First *Silver Pennies,* then *Diego*

*Rivera,* and later *Another Side of Bob Dylan.* She bought that record in a sale bin in the drugstore for less than a dollar, saying he looked like someone I would like. At seventeen it was a seamless transition from Rimbaud to Bob Dylan. Here was another who reinvented the sacred hand of poetry. Even something of their cherubic yet defiant faces mirrored one another. I was certain that *A Hard Rain's A-Gonna Fall* benefited from *After the Deluge* in *Illuminations,* and I could well imagine Rimbaud stretched out in a field listening to *It's Alright, Ma (I'm Only Bleeding).* Both poets' words seemed as if they were written for the tribe of black sheep, outsiders trying to exist in the times they were dealt. Both poets seemed trapped in a static present while perceiving future dimensions folding and unfolding into one another.

In places of higher learning, including the teacher's college I attended, students sat at long tables dissecting Rimbaud or analyzing the tracks of *Highway 61 Revisited.* I failed to join them, not interested in their methods of decryption. No one could wholly discern what Rimbaud or Dylan intended within the layers of *Alchemy of the Verb* or *Desolation Row.* Just as only John of Patmos, despite a thousand interpretations, could fully know the Revelation. I had more presumptive goals than speculating what this poem or that song was about. I desired to inhabit their newfound language, just as I had once longed to eat of the white snake to understand the language of the birds or speak the tongues of afflicted apostles. The Revelator held the apocalyptic key just as Rimbaud held the keys to the savage circus. What if those same keys mystically found their way into Bob Dylan's holy trousers, and after a time, one slipped from his pocket. Might I find it in the dust, trampled by a thousand hooves, the new silver penny.

In dismantling innocence, Peter Pan, Raggedy Ann, and Smokey the Bear are set away in a dusty sanctuary. All the pennies in the world can't buy our Toyland back. The threshold is etched with notches we unwittingly carve ourselves. At nineteen, with little know-how, in my third year in college, I found myself pregnant. Aware of society's severity and the multitude of challenges facing me, I made the first wrenching steps toward the most difficult decision of my young life. In 1966 there was still a terrible stigma attached to unwed mothers and unbeknownst to my family my every waking hour was spent arranging for the well-being of the unborn.

I prayed that I had made the right decision, then called the family together to apprise them of my situation. I knew they pinned much of their faith in me to complete teacher's college, get a position, and help the family. I dreaded delivering a blow to their expectations, but I also trusted in their consideration and tolerance. It's impossible to convey all the conflicting emotions burdening those moments which collapsed into the arms of the moments after. I stood before them, aware of their sacrifices, guidance, and the illnesses they pulled me through. I'm pregnant, I said. I've taken on the responsibility and found a good family for the child. Afterwards, if I am unable to find a factory job I will leave. I stood in the weighty atmosphere of the perplexed silence of my parents' disbelief. My brother crushed his cigarette. So that's what I have to say, I said, then instinctively turned to Todd who had always looked up to me. I'm pregnant,

I repeated, so what do you think of me now? But before anyone could say a word Todd spoke up. He revealed to our collective shock that he too had wrestled with a great personal dilemma. He had secretly dressed in women's clothing for years, and that all the missing pieces of our pathetic wardrobes were hidden in his closet beneath his baseball gear and comic books. He turned and looked at us all squarely, Linda in compassionate silence, our weeping mother, our philosophic but broken father, then fixed his gaze on me. I'm half woman, half man; I'm a transvestite, he said. So, what do you think of me now?

He fell upon his sword for me, deflecting my dishonor. Perhaps I had opened a door for him as well, but I didn't completely grasp the pain of his conflict, how much he had suffered and how he would maneuver his future. There was not a shred of doubt that I had my knight, however dressed, always there, clearing a path before me.

We leave all thought of maps behind, remove the compass from our vest, navigate an alien sea. We separate ourselves and commence to a new world that resists charting. We pocket our own talismans, avowing painful movement, deftly reassembling a delicate timepiece. Another flip of the hourglass, grains spilling over gone paths. Pre-empting the draft, Todd joined the Navy. As Independence Day loomed, I tied my hair back in a loose ponytail, pulled on my coat of art, and somewhat cruelly left my family, my education, the child I bore, and the brambles of God's dwelling place on the edge of Thomas's Field, to pursue a vow I had silently uttered, hardly thirteen years old, in the hall of Picasso.

*My Liberty Dress*

# art/rats

Oh! Our bones are clothed in amorous new flesh.

A. RIMBAUD

I STEPPED OUT OF Port Authority bus terminal with my plaid suitcase. My greatest desire at the time was to surrender as an artist. Perhaps I lacked the necessary skills, but I had the willingness to develop them, for I believed in the truth of my calling and was single-minded in my pursuit to find work. It had come to me as if struck with an ecstatic paralysis. There was no Faustian pact connected with my youthful vows, no expectations from godly elements. In choosing to be an artist I knew I would be on my own, yet still hoped for a compatriot, and providence led me to him.

He was an American boy, raised in a Catholic military family. He had served as an altar boy, excelled in school, played saxophone in the marching band, and achieved an ROTC scholarship to study graphic arts at Pratt Institute. His mother, who favored him, had great hopes that he would enter the priesthood. But his father, who had groomed him for the military, pictured him rising in the ranks with commercial art training to fall back on. He had pale skin, green eyes, and dark curly hair that was cropped close, military style. He was slightly bowlegged and had a natural sailor's gait. In accepting the path his father had chosen for him, he was rewarded with an apartment, shiny knee-high leather riding boots, and a generous stipend. At Pratt he proved himself to be an exceptional draftsman and for a time walked the expected path. No one suspected another self was growing within.

At the age of twenty Robert Mapplethorpe laid down his robes, his saxophone, his boots and rifle. He had experimented with LSD. He looked in the mirror and saw neither a priest nor future captain in the ROTC. He saw himself. The intermittent shuddering that he had felt throughout his life was now undeniable. That shuddering was Art. It was a calling. Gazing in that mirror, he committed himself in an instant, and just as swiftly, all was stripped away. His scholarship, his apartment, his allowance, his shining boots, and, most profoundly, his father's approval. He tapped his thigh and stepped into a new world.

He stayed for a while in a small empty room of a friend's apartment. He slept on a simple white iron bed, surrounded by his portfolios. He slept as Eros with his bow balanced by his side, naked, and no flags covered him. That was the boy that I met in the summer of love. I found my way to him, and he opened his eyes and smiled.

We rescued one another. He had been shunned and disowned. I had the emotional and physical scars of a difficult childbirth. We were one another's buoy, believing in the vows we had made to ourselves. I gave him a silver ring with an anchor; he gave me one in gold with a small stone the color of his eyes. Having little money, we seldom went out at night.

We'd play Tim Buckley records and look at our books on Picasso and Surrealism. On rainy evenings languidly lying together, I'd tell him stories or sing him little songs and he would slowly sit up to have a cigarette, with the sheet to his waist. I would glimpse the changeling aspects of my artist: a fragile sailor, a fleeting coquette, or a young geisha with the smallest touch of rouge on the lips. Perhaps he sensed a duality in me, the tomboy who spurned girlish things, yet had secretly yearned for a Communion dress and veil. On Palm Sunday Robert gave me another kind of white dress, a tattered thing of handkerchief linen, a Victorian girl's undergarment. I slipped it over my head and called it my liberty dress, for it resembled the tunic worn by the woman bearing the flag of the July Revolution in the painting *Liberty Leading the People* by Delacroix.

I look at this same dress now, pinned together, over a hundred years old, already threadbare when Robert found it on a rack of one of the many secondhand places that existed in 1968. Everything imaginable was there, monogrammed shirts, cashmere coats, the finest sheets, silk raincoats, silverware, porcelain cups and saucers, fringed velvets, daguerreotypes, sepia postcards of Europe before the war. Robert and I spent hours in such shops, having little or no money to spend. But one day he went without me, searching for a gift he couldn't afford. It lies in a small LV trunk with a broken latch also found in a thrift store, decades ago on the Bowery. It is discolored like the murals of Florence in the old Caffé Dante by decades of smoke. Discolored by love and neglect, traces of faded blood, rusted safety pins. So much hope and arrogance within a garment so light it can hardly be called cloth folded away like an origami swan.

Emerging from the sweetness of our common cocoon in Brooklyn, Robert and I entered the portals of the Chelsea Hotel. We endured our trials and watched the decade change together, boldly entering the seventies. Though we eventually forged our own paths we never cut the golden thread of our incorruptible bond. Robert immersed himself in photography, seeking to push the boundaries of subject matter yet fully explored in art. He was soon to meet his great companion and future patron Sam Wagstaff, who had a full appreciation of his work. Our room was too small to work in, and I wrote, studied, and observed in the Chelsea lobby. There I crossed paths with many musicians and writers, the most influential being the artist Bobby Neuwirth, Bob Dylan's sidekick in *Dont Look Back*. He read my poems, introduced me to the artists and musicians of the day, and pressed me to write song lyrics.

At the time there was a whirlwind of musical activity at the Chelsea. Robert stayed in a loft close by; I continued living in the hotel with my adventurous new love, the playwright Sam Shepard. He included a couple of my early ballads in his play *Mad Dog Blues*. When I was given the opportunity to read my poems opening Gerard Malanga at St. Mark's Church, I wanted to try something new. Sam suggested I find a guitar player to match the energy of my poems, and I was intrigued by the idea. I had just met the writer Lenny Kaye, who worked at Village Oldies, and he mentioned he played a little guitar. Encouraged by Sam I went back to the record store and recruited him. Lenny never hesitated, if I envisioned a car crash, he replicated one, if I wanted to sing a simple blues song he strummed the chords. Our performance at St. Mark's Church surprisingly garnered much attention, both positive and negative, and led to an offer from the entrepreneur Steve Paul, creator of the infamous club The Scene and manager of Johnny Winter. He wanted me to be the debut artist on his new record label Blue Sky. Envisioning me as a raw, downtown version of Cher, he offered me a lot of money but insisted on complete control of my image and musical collaborators. I was flattered but would never agree to such an arrangement and went my own way.

In the spring Sam and I wrote the play *Cowboy Mouth*. It was slated to debut at the American Place Theatre with Sam and I playing the lead roles. Sam added directions for a section where our characters sparred, improvising a poetic language. I had never improvised onstage, but Sam said not to worry, that it was impossible to make a mistake. His method was simple, yet unforgettable: If you miss a beat, invent another. I took this lesson to heart and it was an invaluable mantra that served every future creative endeavor. I was fortunate to eventually depart the Chelsea emboldened, armed with some upright advice. Sam had encouraged me to break down walls, and William Burroughs steered me, above all, to protect my name, keep it clean.

In 1973 I moved into a small apartment on MacDougal Street across from the Kettle of Fish, the same bar that Kerouac once frequented. It was a time of rapid evolution. During the days I worked part-time in bookstores, and at night I'd sit on the floor of my apartment and write. At times, I'd be driven to go beyond my journal, tack large sheets of paper to the plaster walls and draw with a confidence bordering arrogance. My work became increasingly physical with lines of poems running off the edges onto the plaster. I spewed my poems aloud as a somewhat droll manifesto unfolded across my own small universe: *we are art/rats, filthy pups, words we use up.*

Robert came by one morning with some peyote buttons wrapped in a handkerchief. I was hesitant to misuse a sacred drug, but I trusted Robert and we shared it. Time became meaningless and the morning melted into evening. Where did you go? he asked. I had entered a hollow mountain that had no peak, and a magnificent bird appeared that bled into whiteness. The bird flew to the crest and his noble head, white as snow, became the peak, and I could see within and without. Fifty-two stars fell, faces of destiny, transforming as a pack of cards. And what about you? I asked. Robert smiled. It's all here, I made it for you, and he handed me a physical talisman, a slim length of rawhide knotted and strung with glass beads, a cowboy rosary.

We walked down Bleecker Street to The Pink Tea Cup. Robert ordered pancakes and I had catfish with grits and black coffee. I remember thinking that even under the influence of a sacred drug, he was the artist and I the storyteller. No one thinks as we do, he said, then he went off into the night. I hung the cowboy rosary on a nail next to my bed.

In the evening, perched on the fire escape, always a book on my lap, I read Mrabet, Genet, Cossery, and Paul Bowles. Above the continuous flow of action, I'd keep watch for our modern angels. Art had given us the earliest images of them, winged and androgynous acquainted with the throne of God. An angel appeared to Hagar with comfort, Mary with an announcement, and John of Patmos with the Revelation. Surely, they were still among us, but would they speak to us now? The hope was to reclaim the time when all aspects of knowledge were ever present, not doled out in increments, but swirling in the air we breathe.

I had reoccurring visions of nomads, deserts, and olive groves. I made couscous and slept in my muslin djellaba that I bought at a little Moroccan shop around the corner. I listened to Patty Waters, Albert Ayler, and Pearls Before Swine. I danced alone to the Rolling Stones and the Velvet Underground. I was happy then, everything seemed possible. I performed at La MaMa and acted in Sam Shepard's one-act plays. I liked being onstage, but I was convinced I was no actress. I soon grew tired of the repetition of theater, mouthing the words of another night after night. I preferred writing and speaking my own words. I wrote reviews of records I liked and continued working at Scribner's bookstore. On my lunch breaks I would often visit Andreas Brown, who owned the Gotham Book Mart. He took a liking to my work, published a small book of my prose poems, and presented my first show of drawings in Gotham's small gallery.

At the Chelsea Hotel I had met many poets and musicians. I would see them read at St. Mark's and was invited to read with Jim Carroll and Allen Ginsberg. I was fortunate to read with these two great poets, but I still felt the urge to push further. A friend introduced me to the brilliant and eclectic

Sandy Bull; as a teenager I had listened for hours to his album *Fantasias.* We decided to try something together in a small after-hours jazz club. I read a long piece called *All the hipsters go to the movies,* which I abandoned halfway and just riffed over his intricate patterns on the oud. It was an exhilarating experience; he had inspired and challenged me. Feeling a positive sense of momentum, I haphazardly made my first steps into public life. I chanted and sang my poems, often accompanied by Lenny Kaye on electric guitar, in art galleries, libraries, rooftops, and even a planetarium.

We are not the masters of ourselves, Hermann Hesse wrote. I thought about this for a long time, and decided that it may be true, but we are the masters of our own work. In my mind Bob Dylan remained my model, there was no one I identified with more: his language, his way of walking, his *Tarantula* look, snap tab collar shirt, dark glasses. But I never once felt like him; I always felt like myself. And there were times when I didn't identify with anybody. I'd exercise my personal grunge period, cardigan sweaters over vintage dresses. I'd slip on my combat boots, striding through Washington Square, questioning how should I cast my soul?

Lenny and I were gaining a small, supportive following as we sporadically performed our mix of poetry, three chords and blessed noise, a collaboration that suited us both. Rimbaud served as an unpremeditated directive and wishing to salute the one hundredth anniversary of the publication of *A Season in Hell,* we felt the need to expand musically and searched for a pianist to accompany us. Danny Fields, who had an eye for musical matchmaking, sent us Richard Sohl. Richard was younger than us, with long golden curls like Tadzio in *Death in Venice*. He was intuitive, classically trained, and could play the concertos of Mendelssohn, show tunes, three-chord rock, all with the same insouciant air. Through them, I found and amplified my own voice. I could endlessly sail over Richard's rhythmic chord structures and Lenny was freed up to play interpretively. We became an entity, three to tangle, as Lenny would say.

In 1974 we searched for like minds and found them in Tom Verlaine and Richard Hell, both poets who formed the group Television. They had discovered CBGB, the untapped derelict bar on the Bowery, and the owner Hilly Kristal allowed them to build a small stage. There were no rules, save to be free, no material expectations. We were all striving for the new, merging poetry and rock, stripped down naked, devoid of artifice. In the pursuit of illumination, we may be sullied, but in the pursuit of simplicity, purged; we all sought both.

I was drawn to Tom Verlaine, a disjointed cartoon angel, perhaps the most gifted and beautiful. But youth is intrinsically beautiful, and even through a spotted veil of imperfections, something within startles. Looking back, the burgeoning scene was breathtaking, art rats embracing then breaking apart a vast cultural history, scurrying into the future with speedy and productive energy.

In early June, Richard, Lenny, and I convened at Electric Lady Studios on West Eighth Street only a few blocks from my apartment. It was once the street of artists in the fifties and early sixties. Hans Hofmann had taught in the same building that Jimi Hendrix built his studio and across the way were the ateliers of Jackson Pollock and Lee Krasner. We recorded an independent single, Hendrix's take on *Hey Joe* and *Piss Factory,* a rap drawn from the cruel conditions I experienced as a non-union factory worker in South Jersey. Robert proudly financed three hours of recording, with Lenny producing and Tom Verlaine adding his aggressively inquisitive lead on *Hey Joe*. The single was pressed in Philadelphia, and we sold it for two dollars in the streets, Washington Square Park, Gotham Book Mart, and on the steps of the Metropolitan Museum of Art. In August our trio, supported by Television, played for two weeks upstairs at Max's Kansas City, where I had first seen the Velvet Underground. Slipping in a quarter, Richard selected *Piss Factory* on Max's jukebox. A point of pride for us all.

There was no plan, no design, just an organic upheaval that took me from the written to spoken word. From solitude to collaboration. From the Chelsea to the Caffé Dante to the cabaret stage. One thing tumbled into another. The Wartoke Concern, led by Jane Friedman, became our unofficial management. They provided us with a practice room behind the old Victoria Theatre on the west side of Times Square, the heartbeat of New York City. Lenny, Richard, and I had a place of our own to work on new material. On Rimbaud's passing day we presented Rock n' Rimbaud III in the Roosevelt Hotel adjacent to Grand Central Terminal with a guest appearance of Sandy Bull. Despite the offbeat location people lined around the block, attesting to a mystifying but growing popularity. We then flew with Jane Friedman to the West Coast, playing in clubs and bars, celebrating Rimbaud at Rather Ripped Records.

Our following was fast growing as were our musical ideas and we agreed it was time to expand.

There were heavy rains in mid-December. We held auditions for a guitar/bass player at our practice place. Guarding our core, we wanted someone who sounded like us and wouldn't try to take us in a more conventional direction. Ivan Kral, a gifted refugee from Czechoslovakia, stood apart from all others, most of them refusing to play in a band with a female leader. Hardworking and amiable, he fit in easily with us. Our drills included hours of seamlessly merging poetry with three chords, providing me with an undulant field to riff on and dance. Our first quartet job was at the Main Point outside of Philadelphia opening Eric Burdon. We were all honored to set the stage for the original Animal.

On the first day of spring, we paired with Television and began a five-week stint at CBGB. We played Thursday through Sunday, two sets a night, including Easter and Good Friday. Accustomed to one-off jobs the concentrated residency gave us the opportunity to evolve in real time on stage. The small bar with its pool table and graffitied bathrooms was still under the radar, a locus for those forming new bands and developing new material. No one was documenting success or failure, allowing our arrangements to emerge organically. Having the nightly freedom to go in several directions, we were able to explore the inner world of our songs and the outer reaches of improvisation. Traipsing the curves of the band's yielding flow I excitedly encountered strange tributaries, not afraid of stumbling and simply following Sam's advice when I did.

There were raucous nights and sparse ones. There were sound problems, equipment failures, tears, and small triumphs. Soon our core people followed us downtown. Clive Davis, Lou Reed, and Dave Marsh from *Creem* magazine came to hear both bands as the nights became more electric. Our closing piece was a three-chord landscape, propelled by Chris Kenner's classic *Land of a Thousand Dances*. I was fast developing the misadventures of Johnny, a nod to Robert and a descendent of Burroughs' Johnny from *The Wild Boys*. On a pivotal night, Robert, in his motorcycle jacket, sat with William Burroughs. I could not help but be inspired by their presence, my mentor and muse. By the end of April, for the first time at CBGB they were turning people away.

April 30, 1975, marked the end of the Vietnam War. Activist Cora Weiss and Phil Ochs, whose songs were a mainstay of the anti-war movement, organized The War Is Over, a free celebration in Sheep Meadow in Central Park. On May 11, thousands of people attended the historic gathering featuring advocates Harry Belafonte, Joan Baez, Bella Abzug, and Paul Simon. Phil Ochs had brought everyone together and generously gave space to us, the new upstarts. I wore dark glasses, a frayed white shirt, and a black silk tie. We had never performed to such a huge crowd yet looking out at the sea of people I felt strangely in command. Thousands were sitting on the sloping hills, and as Richard and Lenny struck the clarion chords of *Gloria,* a battlefield littered by the debris of the sixties seemed superimposed over this hopeful gathering. Even in the center of such bittersweet celebration, we mourned the voices raised then dowsed. It was now our generation's duty to rekindle the fiery spirit of our cultural revolution.

At the end of May, we supported WBAI, our great counter-culture radio station, with a free concert broadcast live from a converted church near the Queensboro Bridge. During the improvisational breakdown of *Gloria,* I imparted a brief history of how the four of us came together. At the very end I appealed over the airwaves for a drummer. Jay Dee Daugherty heeded the call and within days we were practicing with him. Less than a month later we made our first public appearance as a rock n roll band, art/rats moving at 78 speed.

On June 26, 1975, we played The Bitter End in the Village, our first performance with a drummer, signaling that we were truly a rock band. The moment I stepped on the stage I knew something was different, the atmosphere exceedingly charged. At first, I attributed it to our expanded sound, but there was something else happening. I could feel it, like high humidity on the skin; the ensuing electricity further igniting our already raucous performance. Afterwards, Bob Dylan entered our dressing room. I heard that unmistakable voice call out—Any poets back here? Filled with adrenaline and inexplicably combative I blurted out—I hate poetry. Considering how much he meant to me, I don't know why I said that, but he just laughed, and nothing seemed more wonderful than seeing Bob Dylan smile. His presence caused quite a stir, and a few people took pictures. The photographer Chuck Pulin asked if he could take a portrait of us together outside by the entrance. When it appeared on the cover of *The Village Voice* a few days later, I was worried what Dylan might think about it. Then I bumped into him on West Fourth Street, outside a newsstand displaying a stack of the paper. He asked me slyly if I knew those two people, and I asked if he was mad. He just shook his head and grinned.

For a time, we lived on the same street, and that summer I would see him walking past my fire escape. We'd run into each other, and sometimes he'd take me wherever he was going. One evening we went to a loft in the West Village. The people were somewhat older, and I felt I was suspiciously observed, but really didn't care. I sat at his feet, and he picked up an acoustic guitar and played every song that would find its way onto the *Desire* album. The one that touched me the most was *One More Cup of Coffee (Valley Below),* that had a kind of Arabic feel. The songs were a blessing to hear, but after a while I grew restless. He was getting ready to play another song when I stood. Are you splitting, he said. Yeah, I said shyly, it's not really my scene.

Bob never seemed offended by anything I said, so I felt free to speak my mind. He'd ask me what I was working on and would tell me his side. I can't say we were friends, but he seemed to trust my opinion about certain matters. He needed a screenwriter for a movie he was planning, and I mentioned Sam Shepard and suggested he call him. Later he asked if I knew any girl singers for his new record.

–Well, I'm a singer, I said.

–No, I mean a real singer.

–You mean I'm not a real singer?

–No, he laughed, I mean you're more like me.

I pretended to be slighted but I was pleased.

In the days to come he talked about creating a kind of vagabond road show and asked me to come to Gerde's Folk City with no explanation. I didn't know what to expect but when I showed up, there was a crowd of well-known musicians, a sense of heightened expectations. Bob was sitting among his people, his wife Sara, Joan Baez, Ramblin' Jack Elliott, and Allen Ginsberg. I gleaned that everyone was expected to do something, perform a poem or sing. I wasn't sure what to do as I didn't play an instrument and had nothing prepared when I heard my name called. I scanned the room, took a breath, and improvised a tale of the madness between an archer and his sister in sixteenth-century Japan. Eric Andersen joined in on guitar. After some faltering, I built a strong rhythm ending with the chant: *I move in another dimension.* There was nothing sublime about it, an entirely primal process but I held my own, proving that I could think on my feet. Then I took off and went crosstown to CBGB, the stronghold of the unknown, to be with my own people.

I could sense a shifting directional energy. Added to that my lease expired, the rent substantially raised, and I was obliged to find a new place to live. I would miss my fire escape overlooking the lively little street, but I was also ready for change. I was called to join the initial gathering of Rolling Thunder Revue in New Haven. I waited in an empty dressing room still uncertain about my duties when Bob entered. He sat down and seemed uneasy. I could tell something was on his mind, so I told him just to spit it out. A lot of people had shown up unexpectedly to play. He said that my slot had to be cut, and that most likely I would be cut from the tour. I admired the fact that he told me himself and did not look away while he was talking. It was fine with me, I knew I didn't fit into their picture, I was too raw and irreverent. I wrapped my long Indian scarf round his neck and wished him luck. Later I would see pictures of him wearing it, like a hello, and that was enough for me. I was proud that he saw something in our band, which I held as a boon through challenging times ahead. His affirmation led others to respectfully circle around us. I didn't join the romping Rolling Thunder but signed with Clive Davis on his new Arista label and soon leapt on a steed of my own.

st. mark's church in-the-Bowery on East Tenth Street has long been a sanctuary for dancers, poets, and activists. It was the historic jewel of my new neighborhood, the site of my first poetry reading; the genesis of my collaboration with Lenny Kaye. I found an apartment close to the church, a sixth-floor walkup with a tub-in-kitchen on East Eleventh Street. Tom Verlaine lived next door, and he helped me move my things, a little worktable, my bedding and portfolios, and all my books and records. I set the mattress on the floor, tacked Moroccan cloths over the windows, arranged my talismans and pronounced it home.

I'd stay up late listening to the Velvet Underground, writing long prose poems. At times I wished that writing was my sole vocation, but some force continued to draw me elseward.

In the morning, I'd go down and buy coffee and chocolate donuts to bring up to Tom. We didn't have telephones, but our kitchen windows faced each other, and we'd call out or just find each other on the street. We both had our bands, part-time jobs, and spent our spare time going to bookstores. We'd linger for hours at the Flying Saucer News Bookstore on Ninth Avenue going through its trove of spiritual and scientific ufology and speculating on the meaning of its huge tin sign that said PROSPERITY CLINIC. We were like ancient children, holding hands and weaving stories merging tales of the Alhambra and alien abduction.

I didn't stray too far east, as at the time there was a lot of hard-drug activity past Avenue B. But within our perimeter was St. Mark's with its dogwood trees and small graveyard, egg creams at Gem Spa newsstand, scrambled eggs and challah bread at B&H, Italian bakeries and early morning vegetable stalls. The East Village was strangely silent late at night, its streetlights mystically artificial as if on a movie set, producing a yearning for something that was yet to happen, something that would stir the senses, that would have the dark pulse of a beautiful arsonist.

Walking home from CBGB one night I saw a red ball sail across an enclosed playground. I thought I heard someone say *catch* but no one was there. Quickly turning a corner, I nearly collided with a lone husky that stopped and stared at me as music streamed from his white eyes. I later hummed fragments of the melody to Lenny. The chords fell to hand as we composed *Free Money,* the first song we wrote together. The lyric, *Scoop the pearls from the sea, cash them in and buy you all the things you need,* was written for my mother. We all wish for things beyond our grasp; she dreamed of having a big house for the family with many bedrooms on a cliff overlooking the Mystic River.

In our practice room tucked away in Times Square we were able to progress at our own speed, within our slow-moving center, while everything surrounding us was moving so fast. Many of our songs evolved playing live then lyrically refined in the practice room, where inspired, I would stop mid-song to write down alternative lines. *Redondo Beach* was originally a poem written in the Chelsea Hotel lobby; Lenny, Richard, and I later developed it as a reggae song. The lyrics for the upbeat *Kimberly,* composed by Ivan Kral, were written to conjure protection for my youngest sibling. Talented, small, clever and adored by my mother, she had a complicated nature and chose a rocky path, though we all did our best to rein her in. *And I feel like some misplaced Joan of Arc and the cause is you looking up at me.* Words that harked back to the memory of holding her in my arms as the old black barn toppled in flames at Thomas's Field.

Having some difficulty transitioning from poetry to lyrics, I turned to Tom, whose own output seemed inexhaustible. He shared one of his methods, randomly opening my notebook to a Promethean dream I had of Jim Morrison, asleep and bound in chains within a marble likeness. In the dream I could feel his life force stirring and cried out *Break it up, break it up Jim, break it up.* Caught in a void of my own I cried until his marble cocoon cracked and split apart; I watched as he emerged winged and flew swiftly into the sky. Mixing stray bits of conversation with lines from my notebook, we crafted the lyrics to *Break It Up,* which Tom simultaneously set to music.

As the band readied our songs for recording, I contemplated our mission, considering what we could offer, raw as we were, to our cultural canon. When young I had romantically embraced the heroic and gleaned that a hero could rise from humble origins. It was now time to harness those young dreams in the unanticipated form of an album. I was the third to be signed to Clive Davis's new Arista label. I left the legalities up to Wartoke but insisted on full creative control of how my work should be presented. There were other labels who expressed interest for more money but only Clive, wholly comprehending my stance, offered the creative freedom I required. This was an exceptional move at the time, especially for a record executive who specialized in making decisions that often resulted in mainstream success. The agreement did result in a few heady arguments, but Clive always kept his word.

Wartoke thought that Paul Rothchild, who had produced the Doors, would be a good fit for me in the studio. We met at the Wartoke office, but it was not a productive meeting. I was sitting on a couch in an old grey trench coat and beatnik sandals when Rothchild, impeccably dressed, entered the room and stood over me. He opened our conversation touting his achievements, that he had made Jim Morrison a star and he believed he could also make me a star, but I would have to let him take full command. I thought it over for a few moments,

*With Richard Sohl, practice room, Times Square*

rose to leave and replied, Jim Morrison was a poet, most likely he created himself.

In the end I chose John Cale, an artist and composer who would make no such claim about his abilities nor demands on his artists. The band admired his musical legacy and appreciated the sound of his solo albums. Unfortunately, we couldn't afford John Wood, his gifted engineer, but Cale agreed to fly from London to New York and take us on.

The day after Labor Day we arrived at the studio that Jimi Hendrix built. Lenny, Richard, Ivan, Jay, and I descended the steps of Electric Lady, past the cosmic space murals lining the halls and entered Studio A, where John Cale was waiting. The fellows spent the entire evening hauling and setting up our equipment. At midnight we recorded our version of *Gloria,* crossing the Van Morrison classic with the poem *Oath* that I had written in 1968. It seemed that every fledgling rock band had covered *Gloria,* but perhaps not a female singer. Tackling it was an initiation of sorts, as well as an answer to those attempting to corner me, or demand self-identification. Richard confidently laid out the opening chords as I half sung the words to *Oath, Jesus died for somebody's sins but not mine,* signaling accountability for my choices in life and art.

*Gloria* was faithful to our live arrangement. I knew very little about recording and wanted to preserve the veracity of a live performance. I was a novice, sometimes unreasonable, desperate to protect our work, suspicious of any changes, excessive overdubbing or suggestions of strings. This led to some contentious moments, but John did his best to satisfy the desire for authenticity while encouraging us to take advantage of unexplored potential within the studio setting.

Lenny called *Birdland* the most incandescent of our musical journey. It had been a mutating piece originally called *The Harbor Song,* a metaphoric voyage of birds in underwater flight, that we performed over Richard's flowing chords. Having no set lyrics it promised to be the album's unscathed improvisation. John found merit in it musically but questioned the idea of winging it lyrically. When I insisted, he challenged me to prove myself. He kept pushing us to reach further as we went through several exhausting takes. I had just read Peter Reich's *A Book of Dreams* and reimagined the scene of his father's funeral; the son believes he sees the lights of his father's spaceship and pleads to be taken with him. Words, no longer my own, expressing the son's transfiguration, generated a kind of phosphorescence. We burned through an emotional field dominated by the boy's desperate cries as Lenny emulated screaming blackbirds on his Fender Stratocaster. John, visibly shaken, finally declared that we had done it. Afterwards, John questioned my origins. I told him I was Irish and English. You're not Irish, he said, you're Welsh, maybe a descendent of a Welsh preacher, which considering John was a Welshman, felt a high compliment.

*Land,* the ten-minute closing piece, stemming from *Land of a Thousand Dances,* was a grueling synthesis of simplicity and improvisational bedlam. Its shifting folds retain the flickering aura of CBGB where it truly evolved. The ever-present figure of Hilly Kristal, the stench of urine and beer, Lizzy Mercier's swinging hair and the faces of the bewildered feverishly spilling onto the Bowery. All were our mirror, exalted and defiled. Johnny, possessing the shining skin of aspiration, negotiates the debris of his century, stretching from an endless hallway to Chris Kenner's dance society to a Portobello vision of a dying Jimi Hendrix, cradled by the pulse of rock and roll. I desired the immediacy of a live performance yet also envisioned Johnny guided and assailed by a chorus of seraphs. We drew up a plan; under John's patient direction I devised several vocal tracks and painstakingly mapped them out. Together we mixed them by hand. These moments of concentrative partnership were the best of a welcomed learning process in Studio A at Electric Lady.

Saluting the departed, *Elegy* was recorded on the fifth anniversary of Jimi Hendrix's death. Flawlessly attentive, Richard accompanied me on piano. In the vocal booth I faltered and couldn't help but wish I was a more accomplished singer, but John and the band encouraged me to continue. The music was written by Allen Lanier, a member of Blue Öyster Cult, who added his ethereal guitar lines. I had envisioned Chet Baker playing the last notes of *Elegy,* but we hadn't the budget for his fee. Yet somehow the call of his trumpet remains within the silent ground of the unattained.

In sequencing the album, I strove, however abstractly, to present the illusion of a cinematic experience. I chose to open with our version of *Gloria,* claiming the right to create, without apology, from a stance beyond gender or social definition, but not beyond the responsibility to create something of worth. The liner notes served as a kind of poetic manifesto. In writing them I thought of my brother, equally torn between two genders. When young I had lamented that I wasn't a boy. It wasn't that I really wanted to be a boy; I wanted the choices that boys seemed to have, but as myself. I wanted freedom and as a child it meant wearing flannel shirts and blue sneakers instead of red, to dress and renounce as I wished. In adolescence, it meant shunning makeup, nail polish, shaving my legs, being groomed for suitable vocations. At twenty it meant defying any predetermined model of feminine behavior set up for us. That is what I resisted, and that is what I fled.

Todd's conflict was quite different. His was the unseen dress. The first slipped from a sister's closet and hidden beneath blue jeans and comic books, forbidden packs of cigarettes and baseball cards. In time a missing blouse and an unhemmed skirt, the dark blue one whose stitches unraveled and was in the sewing pile and then one day just disappeared. None of us were aware that his masculinity wrestled with itself. The pool player with his sports page and cigarette dangling, suddenly overcome with waves of anxiety, the need to slip into the garments of Rachael, the name of Deckard's replicant love in *Blade Runner,* the name he chose for himself. Todd could not flee for Rachael was within him; her female heart beating beneath his ART/RAT tee shirt.

We were brought up in a humanist atmosphere, and the need for openness echoed our parents. I appealed to him to come to New York City, where a far more sympathetic community dwelled, and work with the band. He soon packed his bags and joined our small technical crew and for a time seemed much happier.

In finishing the album there were continuing challenges that were met head-on. There was concern about how I was presenting myself and the art department airbrushed Robert Mapplethorpe's cover photograph, smoothing out my hair and touching up facial idiosyncrasies. I refused any such makeover and confronted Clive; Robert's original image was quickly restored. Keeping an eye on all things I rewrote the ad copy to better suit the band: *three chords merged with the power of the word,* a phrase that was soon to be quoted as much as my lyrics.

I wasn't ungrateful for the opportunity to record but had much to protect. The poet stands alone, but in merging with a band is obliged to surrender to the wonder of teamwork. I now had loyal allies, just as I had experienced when young with my sibling army. Our band had birthed a work together. Despite any failings we held to the desire to forge something new. I understood as we recorded it was not going to appeal to the mainstream, but I felt I could reach out and connect with the fringes of society which was also my society. We hadn't made our record to garnish fame and fortune. We made it for the art rats known and unknown, the marginalized, the shunned, the disowned. It was for the girls grasping the banner, the neo boys of the future, those dropping in from Venus and Mars. I decided on the title *Horses,* taken from *Land*'s improvisation. The horses represented the stampeding current of the world, coming in from all directions, heralding the entrance of Johnny and all the pitfalls and possibilities of youth.

On October 10th we worked through the night mixing *Redondo Beach,* completing our task. As Lenny and I stepped

out into dawn we could not help but reflect how far we had traveled from our first connection at St. Mark's Church. *Horses* was to be pressed in Pitman, New Jersey, at the Columbia record plant where in 1967 I had been unsuccessful in securing a job. My mother's closest friend called her from the plant to say she was slated to press my record. Unfortunately, an oil shortage triggered a vinyl shortage, and the album due October 20th, Arthur Rimbaud's birthday, had to be rescheduled. Clive Davis called personally to inform me as he knew I would be disappointed.

–When will it come out? I asked.

–November 10th is the next available date.

–That's fine, I said. It's Rimbaud's passing day.

–How did you do that!

–I didn't, I laughed, Rimbaud did.

When I first headed to New York I sought to be an artist, but destiny led me to the precipice of public life. In this respect I felt chiefly a worker and believed our struggle a privilege. There were walls everywhere, the cracks were formed by others. All we had to do was kick with all our power, topple them, clear the rubble and create space for the neo rats that I already felt coming. *Horses* signaled freedom, the artlessness of an age. The fellows packed up the equipment, closed our practice room and we took to the road. Wake up! Wake up! Words circling the Earth uttered by another kind of Paul Revere. I had new dark glasses, *charms, sweet angels* stitched on my sleeve. The hyena was showing her wet teeth.

# Dancing Barefoot

Always do what will cost you the most.

SIMONE WEIL

I T WAS THE bicentennial year, 1976, the celebration of the Revolution. We were touring *Horses* riding straight into the future. It was a freewheeling time, hanging out with William Burroughs at his bunker on the Bowery, watching Television at CBGB, plotting a chaotic future with my brother Todd, and crossing America with a rock and roll band. Our country had its great failings, the shame of Vietnam, racial injustice, and sexual discrimination. But we reveled in America's cultural contributions. Rock and roll, jazz, activism, Abstract Expressionism, the Beats. It was a time when I felt my own power and believed in our mission.

Touring *Horses* along the West Coast, we were accompanied by Paul Getty, and the French actress Maria Schneider. Maria, much adored for her performances in *The Passenger* and *Last Tango in Paris,* with intense black eyes and a mass of unruly dark hair, was a mirror in a white shirt and black tie. Paul was the grandson of one of the richest oil magnates in the world and the victim of a famously botched kidnap in Italy. William Burroughs had introduced him to me, a pale acolyte, the youngest passing through his portal of saints. I was quite fond of Paul with his wild red hair, freckled skin, and eyes like mine, slightly cast. William had asked me to keep an eye on him, which was virtually impossible, for Paul was brilliant, intuitive, and reckless. We found like-minded people in San Francisco then spent a few riotous nights playing the Roxy in Los Angeles. The ravenous scene was unique to L.A., devouring as much as it gave. Paul, Maria, and I must have appeared a curious triangle during the band's stay in West Hollywood at the Tropicana Hotel. We all loved it there, it was cheap, gritty, and had seen all kinds of action since the days the Doors recorded *L.A. Woman* just across the highway.

On March 9, 1976, we kissed Maria goodbye and boarded a plane for our first concerts in the Midwest. I wore a black pleated silk dress that Paul had bought me at Bendel's. It was the same dress that Sylvia Kristel wore in the film *Emmanuelle,* only hers was cream. It became my uniform, a five-hundred-dollar dress I paired with my black *Horses* jacket and combat boots.

We landed in Detroit on a windy Tuesday afternoon. The crew left for the Ford Auditorium to set up our equipment and the rest of us went straight to a welcome party hosted by the Detroit musician community at the Lafayette Coney Island. I didn't particularly like parties, but I was lured by their legendary hot dogs and arrived with Paul and the band. The people were very welcoming. We stayed awhile, had their deservedly lauded hot dogs, said goodbye to all, and headed toward the door. That's when I first saw him. He stood by a white radiator in a blue overcoat. I noticed the threads where

a button was missing. That fleeting moment was to redirect
the whole of my life. Lenny introduced us simply: Fred Smith
Patti Smith, Patti Smith Fred Smith. He had lank brown hair
and eyes like water. He placed the button in my hand, and I
wordlessly declared it treasure. I felt a gravitational force; my
being truly shaken, kindling my desire for the One, the better
savage. Fate had touched us; I knew in that moment he was
the one I would marry.

Soon after we checked into the hotel, Paul gathered his
things and bid me farewell. When I asked him why he was
leaving he looked straight into me and said you and that guy
are meant to be together. I feebly answered that I didn't even
know him but truthfully could hardly protest. He smiled as he
left, Paul with his pale freckled skin, one ear, and long tangle
of red hair, a fallen clairvoyant archangel.

FRED SONIC SMITH was born in West Virginia in his grandfather's kitchen. His small and feisty grandfather, once a coal
miner, delivered him because the midwife was unable to get
there in time. Fred's mother was intensely religious. His father
was a rough and ready teamster who loved Bill Monroe and
knew every Hank Williams song. Good natured and hardworking, he had harbored a mean streak; father and son often
physically clashed from the time Fred was a boy.

In high school Fred was extremely athletic. His boxing
coach was impressed with his defensive agility and long reach.
But privately aware of his suppressed rage, Fred bowed out,
fearing he might hurt someone. He was also scouted by the

*Fred with his grandfather, West Virginia*

Tigers' farm team because of his tremendous throwing arm. He was overjoyed but conflicted, for at the same time he was co-forming the band that was to become the revolutionary MC5. At sixteen he fled from home, school, sports, and the draft. Wielding his guitar as his weapon, Fred's conflicting emotions dominated his playing. When we first met, I had no idea who he was, but I knew instantly he would be my life. Such is the terrible mystery of love, that draws us from all that we know.

I didn't see him again until December, after our second concert in Detroit. Our band and crew joined local musicians at the bar in the Renaissance hotel. Fred took my hand, and we slipped away, entered the scenic glass and steel elevator, and he pressed the twenty-fifth floor. Those moments in the slow-rise elevator were our first alone together, and I can still recall the intense beating of my heart. With the panorama of the Motor City growing distant below, our far-off courtship began, one that would depend more on trust and patience than actual presence. Letters, telepathic wishes, and occasional phone calls at a time when long-distance calling was prohibitively expensive. On tour in some obscure town spying a phone booth, I would pocket everyone's change, stop our tour bus by the side of a road, and call, even for a few minutes, just to hear his voice.

Though it kept us apart the opportunity to tour the world was a blessing for the penniless traveler. So many pages from *Around the World in 1,000 Pictures* turning. Yet nothing had prepared us for the response of the young in Brussels, London, Paris, Amsterdam, Germany, all over Europe. Lenny and I spent as much time as possible talking with kids that gathered outside our hotels, in the streets, or standing in line before a concert. We answered their questions, encouraging them to start their own bands. We happily collided with known and yet unknown members of rising new bands: Siouxsie Sioux, members of the Slits and the Clash.

Sonic's Rendezvous Band was touring on the other side of the world. Fred and I saw each other when we could; in the early days of our courtship I would fly to Detroit, even for two days to be together. The closer we got the more he seemed to test my faith in him. When we left his car to have tires changed, we took a brief walk along the highway. He stopped and held out his hand. Do you trust me, he asked. Yes, I said, taking his hand as he led me halfway across the road. I let him take me in his arms, closed my eyes, and waltzed with him. Even as the traffic intensified, we continued to dance unharmed on the median. At an abandoned reservoir we navigated a stony path in the available moonlight. Looking up, Fred raised his hands toward the stars and seemed to rearrange them, bringing them closer, and turning them in his hands. These moments felt like hours, yet were mere seconds, our minds as one. We did not speak of them; we lived them. Fred could be abstract, futuristic, with the hands of a musician, a mathematician, a magician.

More than ever my writing life was usurped, living fiercely in the present, tour upon tour, a physical external time when the writer deferred to the performer, the pen to the electric guitar. For a time, I lost contact with language; my Fender Duo-Sonic spoke for me, moaning and screeching feedback in place of words. I felt somewhat conflicted at the sight of my journals, containing little else save scattered lyrics and abandoned letters to Fred. Rimbaud had proclaimed himself scourge and seer, advancing then intentionally shooting himself in the foot, then walking upright. My feet were riddled with imaginary holes. I felt a walking contradiction negotiating a desire to stand still yet compelled to race into the future. Todd was always by my side. Throughout childhood, he stepped back allowing me to take on the roles of hero, general, king, always being the dedicated first soldier, first knight.

I embraced my responsibility as the leader, but one who broke bread with her troops, accessible to the crew and the people. As the band evolved, Todd was declared HOC, head of crew; our years of play had prepared us for our roles. Todd carried out orders, transporting guitars, amplifiers, and delivering late-night reports. On our nights off I would watch with pleasure as he'd chalk the end of his pool cue, cigarette dangling, and with his ice blue eyes fixed on a ball, clear the table to the admiring curses of his opponents. On the road I carried the *Seven Pillars of Wisdom,* mapping out our campaign. Todd prepared my way, magnifying my position of the weary field marshal. We negotiated rapturous crowds, the swarms of kids calling to us outside our hotels at night. Sometimes after a concert we'd all gather in my room, laughing until dawn about nothing. It wasn't happiness, but something at the time that seemed more intoxicating; it was abandon.

In between tours, we were called to take a break and make another record. I hadn't banked on a follow-up to *Horses* and struggling to write lyrics for another album I laid out the things that were on my mind: famine in Ethiopia, the fate of a boxer, Rimbaud in Abyssinia, and the sonic language of the electric guitar. I received a letter from a girl named Andi Ostrowe, who had read that we were about to record *Radio Ethiopia*. She had recently returned from the Peace Corps serving in a southern rural village in Ethiopia. We met up and talked of the current revolution, the deposing of Haile Selassie, the destructive military coup, and the city of Harar where Rimbaud had been a coffee trader. She was small and sincere with dark hair and dark eyes. I was moved by her pictures and keepsakes from the country I had yearned to journey to and promised to invite her to the studio.

I chose Jack Douglas to produce the album believing he was a good match for both sides of the band's personality. We could be unrestrained and at times incomprehensible yet benefited by Ivan's relatable song structures: *Ask the Angels* was written for a thriving network of kids off the grid with a special nod to the youth of Los Angeles. The reggae inspired *Ain't It Strange* was a confrontational invitation to an impossible dance. The emotional *Pissing in a River* swerved from referencing the past to interrogating the future. The greatest challenge was our title track which I envisioned as entirely improvisational, primarily driven by Lenny's churning riff then veering into the seemingly unattainable. I urged the band to take the impassioned risks I so admired in the work of Albert Ayler and Ornette Coleman. We made a few passes but not satisfied we all agreed to wait and try again.

On August 9th, Jack grounded us as a hurricane was fast approaching New York City. I paced the floor like a hemmed-in coyote feeling the effects of both the coming storm and the full moon and was swept by a premonition that we would get the title track that night. I called Jack and after a short standoff he headed to the city during the first throes of Hurricane Belle. Todd rounded up the band and I packed my Duo-Sonic, called Andi, and we all met at the Record Plant. Jack wedged towels under the control room doors in case the heavy rains caused flooding. At midnight, the deluge peaking, we plunged together into the well of our most ambitious undertaking. I had no words, just a mental map of the sufferings of a people, the death rattle of one of our greatest poets, and the desire for us to unleash a torrent of our own. Midway Lenny's Big Muff pedal crashed, a true disaster as it was the core of his sound. It turned out that Andi played guitar and had a Muff; she braved the weather and saved the day. By three in the morning four inches of rain had come down flooding the streets, high winds had knocked over trees and power lines, and we had successfully added to nature's chaotic touchdown. Twelve minutes of propelling distortion, Jay Dee's thundering drums and splashing cymbals, Ivan's pumping bass, and as my whining Fender Duo-Sonic drew altruistic swords with the mournful wailings of Lenny's Stratocaster, Richard Sohl introduced an unexpected melodic shift creating the melancholic beauty of Abyssinia. Through it all the thread of our collective consciousness had not snapped as intentional babbling channeled famine in Ethiopia, the mallet and hard arms of the sculptor Brâncuşi, and the last words of Arthur Rimbaud.

Jack's willingness to defy the storm and unlock the studio allowed us to generate our title track, which accomplished all that I had hoped for. With her Leica, the photographer Judy

Linn shot the image of me in a dark silk raincoat and my hair in a ponytail for the cover. She perfectly captured my frame of mind and the gritty atmosphere of our practice room. In solidarity with the band, I added *group* to my name. Andi lent her pictures for the album insert and wrote my catchwords *the tongue of love* in Amharic. She was soon hired as Todd's technical assistant, a welcomed addition to our small and loyal crew, ready to tackle any task that came to hand.

*Radio Ethiopia,* released nearly a year after *Horses,* was not well received and the title track I was so proud of was deemed unlistenable. Some of our former champions accused us of selling out and Jack Douglas was picked apart, blamed for supposedly changing our direction. We were energetically evolving, and I was certainly no pawn. Jack drew from us what we had desired and were intent on giving, flawed and unruly as we were. Compounding all woes *Pissing in a River* was surprisingly chosen as a single. I was requested to change the lyric to swimming or wading in the river. I hadn't considered that the word *pissing* would cause such a stir, but would not change the lyric, and it received only limited bleeped airplay.

There were arrows everywhere, but I took it in stride, rallying our camp with a message from the liner notes: *The art emerging from the boundless scope of rock n roll needs no other patron but the people.* With that in mind we plunged back into touring starting in Stockholm broadcasted on Swedish TV. One of the most memorable concerts was in Spain. The former fascist regime had denied two things from Spanish culture: Picasso's *Guernica* and rock n roll. With the death of Franco, Picasso's masterpiece, his response to the horrors of war, was installed in Madrid. And on Rimbaud's birthday we were flown from Paris to Barcelona by the bold and idealistic promoter Gay Mercader for a makeshift concert. We used whatever equipment was on hand, and that night we all danced in celebration, spawning a lifelong kinship with the Spanish people.

In December we returned to the States and played the Tower Theater in Upper Darby, not far from Rambo Terrace where we had stayed with our contentious Aunt Gloria in 1949. I could see my mother, who thrived on the energy of our concerts, in the front row surrounded by her own adoring fans. As Lenny's downstrokes introduced the continually amending misadventures of Johnny, I caught sight of wide stretches of the American plain. Wild horses with lightning bolts tattooed on each ear raced through the dust as we segued into *Gloria*. As I left the theater with my mother a horde of kids surrounded me with albums to sign. It was cold, and I felt wired and exhausted and wanted to keep going. My mother was incensed that I would walk away from them. You sign every album, she demanded, don't forget who put you here.

We relentlessly toured *Radio Ethiopia;* I felt ready for a break and planned to see Fred in Detroit. We were asked to add two more dates at the end of our already demanding schedule to play with Bob Seger in Florida. I reluctantly agreed as it was a beneficial challenge. On the first night we were dismissively given very little light or space to work with. The stage was high and having height phobia I had trepidation about the next job, with a higher stage. I called Fred for advice, and he offered to call Seger himself, but I felt it was my duty to approach him on my own. Just tell him how you feel, Fred advised, he's from Detroit, he'll do the right thing. Though I could sometimes come across as caustic, I carefully chose my words and needs for some extra space and light. Seger had little to say, seemed bemused and walked away.

Before we took the stage, my brother was highly agitated. Todd had given us less than two feet extra, but the Seger crew reset our equipment and barred him from the stage until we went on. Todd looked worried and told me to be careful. I was a very physical performer but did my best to hold back, though hazy lighting made it difficult to discern the stage's edge. The seventh song *Ain't It Strange* was our most dynamic and as always, I spun Dervish-like stopping myself by firmly planting my foot on my floor monitor. Only Seger's crew had repositioned my monitor partially off the edge of the stage, so when I hit the monitor with my foot it tumbled, and I went over head and shoulders first. My brother quickly leapt to the ground after me. I will never forget the look in his eyes as he cradled my bleeding head. In the hospital emergency ward, they cleaned the gash in my head without any anesthetic and proceeded to give me forty stitches. Just keep thinking Civil War, Todd kept saying, think of what those soldiers endured on the battlefield, just keep thinking Civil War.

I suffered a skull fracture, a severe concussion, and four spinal fractures. My management demanded that I sue the Seger organization, but the idea of being compensated by financial gain morally repelled me. It was a stance held by my parents and how I operated. However, it was wrongfully reported that I was so stoned that I danced off the stage. I was unable to defend myself as I was completely incapacitated. Rendered helpless to do his job, Todd was devastated by my fall.

At the time I still lived in my sixth-floor walkup in the East Village, so it was impossible to return. I spent my immobile months with a neck brace in the apartment with an elevator I had once shared with Allen Lanier, who was on a lengthy tour with Blue Öyster Cult. Having no medical insurance, I was tended to round the clock by my own people. Andi Ostrowe took care of my personal needs. Robert looked in on me every day and Sam Wagstaff generously took care of any medical bills. Tom Verlaine brought me books I was unable to read because of blurred vision but I kept them by me. On one occasion the Ramones brought me a small bottle of tequila in a brown paper bag and a copy of *Punk* magazine with two drawings of me on the cover. Joey Ramone stood at the foot of my bed, long hair, glasses, and torn dungarees. We talked about the genesis of the word punk and how it was being redefined from the negative to the positive. An action I had been deeply thinking about, the transformation of the connotation of certain words.

During my lengthy convalescence I examined where I was in life, what my future looked like. Though the accident was not of my doing, a part of me imagined it as a shadow of a divine warner. William Burroughs visited with a fish wrapped in newspaper and made us a meal. He drew a chair next to my bed and questioned me about the accident and I confessed my thoughts. William told me that a terrible accident had made him a writer and spoke of the line between practical facts and atmospheric or mystical intervention.

I would come to examine the positive aspects of my fall as well. Despite damage to my sight and altered physical abilities, my consciousness unfolded like a bright scroll, and I reconnected with the mystic flow of language, the golden scales of heroic deeds. With Lenny's assistance I orally created the long prose poems that would comprise my first major book of poetry. Our friendship and years of improvising live allowed me to dictate without self-consciousness as he speedily transcribed on my Hermes 2000. I titled the book *Babel* foreshadowing some of the themes of our next album: the pursuit of a new language, professing devotion, and my horizontal attempt to open the wounds of poetry.

Toddy and I watched TV together on a small black-and-white that Sam Wagstaff provided. We discovered *Star Trek* during a marathon of reruns. Captain Kirk directing his crew fueled my impatience to reclaim my role as leader. *Movie of the Week* showed one obscure film continuously. *The Gospel According to St. Matthew* aired from Palm Sunday through Easter. I watched it alone many times, mesmerized by the aesthetic beauty of Pasolini's documentary style, faithful to the Gospel. Pasolini presented the Messiah clearly as a revolutionary whose teachings were based on love, reawakening me to the original intentions of Christ.

My neck brace was made of plaster, heavy and uncomfortable. Sam brought in a specialist to replace it with a detachable cervical collar of sturdy foam. I removed it once so Robert could take a photograph. He was pleased with the image, an arresting capture of fear and determination. Though I had trusted him I felt exceedingly exposed without it. I realized it would take some time before I could maneuver normally or travel. When Fred flew in from Detroit to see me, I was excited at the prospect but reluctant for him to see me in my cervical collar. He sat by me and deftly removed it himself, and it remained off for several minutes. I felt reassured in his presence and for the first time felt the possibility of removing it for good.

Eventually we must act, set in motion a process that will push us closer to the open wound. Entering the fourth month of immobility, spending precious time with Fred, I was hungry to be whole again. Sam Wagstaff was friendly with Arthur Allen Jones who pioneered resistance training and arranged for me to enter his Nautilus Institute for Sports Medicine. As a non-athlete and the sole female, I was fortunate to be offered this opportunity and wholeheartedly complied, yielding to their rigorous program. Though the prospect of returning to the stage was daunting, intense physical therapy readied me for the task. Billed as Basic Training, we had a short run at CBGB. I performed in my neck brace while Toddy and Andi crouched on the side of the stage, eyes on my every step. I was happy to be in familiar territory, but I was also cautious and stayed close to the microphone as if an ally. The people packed the club every night, and despite my immobility greeted us with a warm show of support.

It's difficult to convey all the rapid changes of this period of my life. The balancing act of grueling rehabilitation, my deepening feelings for Fred, and the intoxication of writing poetry.

At times I was consumed with polarizing visions of the future. In working on *Babel,* I again craved the solitude to write, to materialize with words the secrets of the world. But performing, however limited, stoked the urge to get back in action, join forces with the brethren, slinging electric guitars in lieu of weapons.

I slowly ventured out still in my collar. William invited me to accompany him to Gotham Book Mart to celebrate the reissue of *Junkie* with Allen Ginsberg and Carl Solomon. Later he asked if I would play the part of Mary in *Junkie*'s screen adaptation and introduced me to his somewhat eccentric producer. Jacques Stern, also known as Baron Rothschild, had suffered polio and got around in a motorized wheelchair. His legs were covered with a throw that would occasionally slip revealing them as slight, withered. His brown hair fell around his sharply angled face, reminding me of Artaud. Jacques commissioned Terry Southern to write the screenplay. Dennis Hopper would play the part of Bill Lee, the narrator of the novel. We would all meet up at the El Quijote bar adjacent to the Chelsea. It was a strange window I was glimpsing through. I'm sure I seemed somewhat odd myself, a girl wearing a neck brace not drinking, smoking or ingesting drugs. But William had chosen me; Mary was the only female part.

When everything was agreed upon, we celebrated at Jacques's spectacular apartment off Gramercy Park. Propelled by his wheelchair, Jacques led me to his study and handed me the key to an old trunk supposedly filled with Artaud's letters. At that moment an extremely fashionable woman burst through the double doors screaming. It turned out the

baroness had returned from Europe, immediately threaten-
ing to commit Jacques to an institution and berating William
for running through their money. We were quickly thrown
out and the film was shut down before it began. I can still see
William shaking his head and shuffling the streets with his
hands in the pockets of his overcoat. I never saw Jacques again
but dedicated a long poem to him called *Ha! Ha! Houdini!* that
Gotham Book Mart published with its own tiny lock and key.

I was on a stationary bike at Nautilus, the tension was set much
higher than usual and I nearly vomited from the effort. I was
aware that my strength was being tested and successfully kept
going. It was August 16th and the song on the radio was inter-
rupted by the announcement that Elvis Presley had died. I can't
say why but I felt an irrational rage at the core of my sorrow. He
was only forty-two and despite his great fame was much
maligned and misunderstood. I felt an all-consuming urgency to
break out and get back into action. I bid a grateful farewell to
Mike O'Shay my patient trainer and left the Sports Institute.
The weather was good. Advised to take long walks I tread two
and a half miles to the East Village. I stopped to visit the French
artist Lizzy Mercier, a wild little thing who loved Rimbaud.
Without hesitation I removed the neck brace and let it drop to
the floor. Lizzy provided the lighter and I set it on fire.

The band continued to play locally. Through months of
Nautilus training, I had grown physically stronger, yet I had
become somewhat guarded onstage. At summer's end Richard,
Andi, and I took the subway to Coney Island. Richard per-
suaded me to brave the roller coaster with him, hoping to melt

away my last vestiges of physical trepidation. It was a harrowing though exhilarating experience, a giant step toward proceeding without fear.

I was still not cleared for lengthy travel, so we prepared to make another record. When we last recorded at the Record Plant, I befriended a scrappy Italian kid named Jimmy Iovine who engineered for Bruce Springsteen. I admired his focus and tireless work ethic and called upon him to produce our album. The choice of an unknown with no production credit was not well received by Arista but I believed he was exactly the right person. I still felt somewhat vulnerable and sensed I could depend on him, as producer and protector. Toddy and Jimmy had immediate chemistry and worked perfectly as a technical team.

After months of inaction, we had little material and constructed our album song by song. Pages of unfinished lyrics, poems, and manifestos against censorship covered the floor of our practice room, touching on spiritual alchemy, the transformation of waste, redemption, and the redefining of words. Lenny's rousing *Till Victory* served as an announcement that we were back. We wrote *Ghost Dance* in memory of the Hopi tribe's resurrection dance. I had written *We Three* as a slow dance recalling the earliest nights at CBGB. Ivan's incendiary *25th Floor* revisited my first romantic encounter with Fred at the top of the Renaissance hotel in Detroit, opening an electrifying path for layers of feedback and cascading imagery.

Mid-recording Richard became ill, and it was advised that he take a long break. I was distressed to lose him but reassured him that he could return as soon as he was ready. Ivan brought the musician Bruce Brody into the fold. He had worked with John Cale, was exceptional at the keyboards, handled the delicate situation with respect, and worked well with Jimmy and the band.

I had decided to call the album *Easter* and wrote lyrics for the title track but had no melody in mind. I pictured the Rimbaud siblings being marched to church in a row by their mother and the resentful child poet's mystical escape into a celestial tolling of bells. One afternoon I arrived at the practice room early, Jay Dee was already there, not at the drums but at the keyboard playing an unworldly piece of music, the perfect complement to my lyrics. *Easter* was the first song we wrote together.

Jimmy spared me of the fact that he was under tremendous pressure to prove himself to Clive Davis. He was close with Bruce Springsteen and remembered a song that he had abandoned, unhappy with the lyrics. At his request Bruce gave him a work tape for me to hear. Jimmy was insistent that I listen to it, but I desperately wanted the album to be our own material, and we had already recorded an emotional cover of *Free Me* from the film *Privilege*. I placed the cassette on my mantel, stubbornly passing over Jimmy's persistent pleas to listen to it.

Because long-distance calls were so expensive, Fred and I would have one phone call a week, the same day and appointed hour. Fred was late in calling. I paced, made coffee, and tried to distract myself as the hours passed. As my restlessness mounted, I spied the cassette on the mantel and to appease Jimmy I listened to it. Instantly I recognized its potential. It was in my key, inherently sensual with a relentless immediacy.

It's a darn hit, I said to myself. Fred finally called around mid-night. By then, not able to resist the musical artistry of Bruce, I had written the lyrics *Have I doubt when I'm alone, love is a ring, the telephone* as a love song for Fred.

*Because the Night* was the last song we recorded. Under Jimmy's direction we approached it anthemically. There was no question in my mind that we had been given a gift and in turn served it well. I was enveloped by a strange cloud as Jimmy and Shelly Yakus mixed our album. I still possessed the extreme adrenaline that had driven me as a performer, yet I found myself yearning to be somewhere else, where nature regenerates with the glistening energy of a fairy tale. A place where one might encounter Fionn the warrior poet or one's true love. That state of mind manifested rebirth, perfectly illuminated in the title track, ascending into a cacophony of bells and bagpipes.

*Easter* was released on March 3, 1978, to favorable reviews. The cover photograph was taken by Lynn Goldsmith. We had enjoyed an interactive flow as we shot many pictures in her studio resonating spring and the colors of a child's Easter. But in the end, I gravitated toward a more energetic image. Wearing a woven silk camisole, my bared arms were raised as I adjusted my bobby pins, an unconscious action impossible before physical therapy. We were both stunned by the intense critical reaction to my scant amount of armpit hair and certain record stores declined to display it. It was taken as an act of defiance, but I had never shaved, and I chose the image as it possessed the vitality of my present state.

I gave my motorcycle jacket to Jimmy, my faith in him

magnified by his own achievements. After being grounded for nearly a year we went back on the road. Fred had given me two of his most precious garments, a vintage green and white checkered vest and a frayed MC5 tee shirt. They became, with a worn buckskin jacket, my uniform of return.

We boarded a train from Germany and arrived in Paris on Easter morning. For the occasion I wore my black silk dress and heavy work boots. My physical abandonment as a performer had been temporarily wrenched by fate; I had lost some of my dexterity and could no longer do a backbend with my guitar, yet never felt sturdier. Internally though, I wrestled with an unexpected dilemma. Even as I embraced stepping back in the world, surrounded by my loyal band and crew, I felt myself detaching. The energy I had returning to the stage was unbelievable, yet at times I would feel displaced, suffering a degree of humility that challenged my former effortless irreverence. In performing *Gloria,* the eyes of Pasolini and his view of Jesus as a revolutionary haunted me. My opening lines from a poem written at twenty were not expansive enough for current aspirations. It wasn't that I wished to recant my former words, it was simply that I had evolved past them. I also understood that the work I had transcended was meaningful to others. This was a new balancing act, between needs and expectations and my burgeoning new code.

Being back to work, immersed as head of crew was good for my brother. He flourished under the weight of welcomed responsibility and spoke little of his inner conflicts. He had met a beautiful artist named Tara in our travels who was sturdy and open-minded, and he was able to express himself fully with her. Having worked with other bands, she soon joined the crew as Jay Dee's drum technician.

Our new material was liberating, and the public greeted us with unrestrained enthusiasm. The band would celebrate, I would return to my room alone happy to find a simple message slipped under my door: Mr. Smith called. I would close my eyes and feel his presence. Before we headed home, we stopped in Manchester where we performed *Because the Night* followed by *25th Floor* live on *The Old Grey Whistle Test* for BBC TV. I threw myself into the performance, Duo-Sonic in hand, with much of my old ferocity. The song was a hymn to my guitar activating radar toward Detroit. I loved my guitar; it never failed to inspire a heightened physicality. Its heavy strings were like barbed wire that I could rip out in one yank. Even Fred could not do that.

It hadn't been a long tour, but I was anxious to head home as I had much work to do. Robert Miller had offered me an exhibition of my drawings at his Fifty-Seventh Street gallery. I requested that it be a dual show with Robert and he agreed. I created much new work on the road, taping drawing paper side by side with Robert's photographs on the hotel walls, responding with my own interpretation. On a break we created the twelve-minute film *Still Moving* to project in the gallery. He installed a framework entirely of white net save a bronze statue of Mephistopheles. To be free to shoot stills he recruited the gifted young Lisa Rinzler for the camera work. I walked into the frame of his mind with my Swiss Army boots, Fred's clothing, and my tattered liberty dress. Robert made me a long length of white leather tied with small white feathers, a ghost dance necklace to wear with it. My monologue was purely improvisational morphing masculine and feminine elements, shifting from the white dress to my performing clothes. At one point I reached out to tear down the cocoon-like net he had hung. I had blindfolded myself with a ragged piece of cloth and couldn't find the edge. Robert reached for me; a close-up of his prominently veined hand firmly encircling my wrist was the perfect unifying moment.

We courted the invisible together, just as we had both embraced the concept of God as children. The artist seeks the infinite, yet creates on earth, attempting to snatch a wisp of the consciousness of God, then returning to create material things. We saw this as an inherent sin in the contract of the artist. Our exhibition was the pinnacle of our decade of collaboration. Sam Wagstaff generously framed the work. My drawings framed in gold leaf had the aura of illuminated manuscripts. Robert's large portraits of me were breathtaking. Holding my neck brace, cutting my hair, blindfolded grasping white net, discreet nudes by the ribs of a radiator. *Still Moving,* projected on the white wall, felt a definitive achievement. Robert Miller held a reception at his home off Central Park. I was standing next to him when his bell rang. It was John Lennon and Yoko Ono, saying they were unable to come to the party but had seen the exhibit. Yoko smiled, and John looked at me and said, *Good work*. It was my sole encounter with him, words I held as an amulet for the future.

*Because the Night* was a global success. It climbed to number thirteen on the Billboard charts, but my resistance to accept certain promotional appearances most likely held it back. My refusal to lip-synch the song on Dick Clark's national television show cost us the success he had promised if I agreed. I could not bring myself to comply, to lip-synch seemed the height of hypocrisy. The single quickly slid off the charts; it appeared I had been somewhat naive in believing one got successful solely by their own merit.

We returned to Europe where we enjoyed unparalleled artistic freedom. To Wales the country of the ancient Celts, Merlin, and Dylan Thomas. To Germany where the young crawled in the dark to spread graffiti across the Berlin Wall. To Vienna waltzing with the spirits of Wittgenstein, Mozart, and Harry Lime. We traced the steps of our heroes and in moments of communal intoxication discarded them one by one.

IN THE DELACROIX museum in Paris there hangs the artist's rendering of Mary Magdalene. Nothing is as rich as the simplicity of the human face, intrepid, unadorned, more awash with light than loss. With head cocked, she gazes up to her crucified Master. Her face imparts hope and despair. The Master has touched her forehead, she sees as he sees, humankind will run amok a thousand times in his name. I stood before the portrait, a humble masterpiece, promising to write a song for her that was also for myself. I tacked a postcard image of the Magdalene inside my guitar case for inspiration and slowly wrote verses of a yet untitled song.

In October we spoke of making another record. I knew in my heart it would be our last. Richard had thankfully returned to our open arms in good health. The two of us took a ferry to

Staten Island and went to the ocean. It was a bit chilly, and he sat wrapped in his raincoat on the shore as I walked up and down alone writing a little song I called *Frederick,* feeling him fast asleep somewhere in Detroit, sad to be so far away but happy that he existed. I had the words and melody and as we boarded the ferry back, I sang it to Richard. He surprised me a few days later in the practice room by playing a variation of *Frederick* on the piano, a danceable lullaby.

Lenny and I wrote a small hymn that he played on his Autoharp. He also set music to a poem I had written a decade before in opposition to colonial rule. It was a strange little poem that he transformed as an anthemic farewell. Ivan and I wrote *Citizen Ship* which merged his experience in 1968 as a refugee from Czechoslovakia with the political and cultural unrest in America. Ivan gave me a cassette tape with some song ideas, guitar riffs, and melodies. One piece led to *Dancing Barefoot,* the song I pledged to write when gazing at Mary Magdalene's face in the Delacroix museum. Having the music, I sketched out a three-tiered lyric encompassing devotion to the people, one's chosen love, and our Creator.

With Jimmy in great demand, our friend Todd Rundgren agreed to produce *Wave.* He worked out of Bearsville Studio where he had recorded Meat Loaf's *Bat Out of Hell* and his own solo albums. We all stayed together in the living quarters upstairs from the studio, sleeping on couches and bunkbeds, while Richard slept on the professional-size pool table. Andi took care of our practical needs while Toddy and Tara stayed in the city working with the Skafish crew at Hurrah. Being isolated in the dead of winter in Woodstock was logistically problematic; we were sometimes snowed in, making it impossible to travel. I had one foot in Detroit, one in New York, both often stranded in Bearsville.

In early December Sid Vicious attacked my brother in Hurrah shoving a broken bottle in his face, narrowly missing his eye. Toddy got seven stitches and pressed charges solely to get him safely locked up, suggesting to the police that he be placed under suicide watch. Unfortunately, he was soon released from jail and two days later he was dead. These things were on my mind when we recorded the Byrds' *So You Want to Be a Rock 'n' Roll Star*. We tore through it propelled by Jay Dee's thundering salute to Keith Moon. In the breakdown I projected Toddy's bloodied eye, the mortification of Sid Vicious, and pondered the future of rock and roll as an art form.

It is with improvisation that we seek to transcend the recording medium. We had developed the confessional *Seven Ways of Going* as a live piece. Todd, feeling he wasn't required at the helm, left us to ourselves: Lenny on guitar, myself on clarinet. Richard on RMI, Ivan on bass, Jay on drums, and Andi on timpani. Propelled by the band's aural maelstrom I was able to cast out the conflicting emotions that had plagued me in the aftermath of my fall. The band wrestled with the track through the night until we were no longer separate entities, surrendering, in the wake of Richard's moving coda, to love, the ineffable miracle.

In the morning, we recorded the title track, which I improvised on piano. Richard produced the sound of the ocean on synthesizer, while Ivan added a sense of the immaterial voice

of the Pope on cello. It was a spoken piece, a child encounter-
ing Albino Luciani, Pope John Paul I, on a windy beach.
Though he died only thirty-three days after being appointed, I
had grown fond of him for his pure nature and his affection
for Pinocchio. The child thanks him for his smile that fills her
with happiness then waves goodbye. *Wave,* a conversion to my
original being, would close the album.

Robert shot the cover photograph in Sam Wagstaff's
sparsely furnished apartment where we had taken the *Horses*
cover. I wanted to wear white, but my liberty dress was in such
fragile condition that Toddy found me another in a thrift store
in Austin, Texas. One white dove, a reference to a line in
*Frederick,* rested in my hand, another circled and landed upon
the finger that points the way. They seemed to represent what
I had sought and what I now was seeking.

The completed album was held up while I sparred with
Arista over the lyrics in *Dancing Barefoot.* There was a deep
concern about my use of the word heroine, and I was asked to
change it for the sake of radio play. I assured everyone that it
was not a drug reference, but the feminine version of hero and
her sole intoxication was that of a love that eclipsed fame and
fortune. I held my ground, the lyric remained and *Dancing
Barefoot* received little airplay in America.

In June we flew to Chicago for a last job before our break,
a double bill at the Aragon Ballroom with Sonic's Rendezvous
Band. I was overjoyed at the opportunity to have us all play
together, but as we slept our Ryder truck was stolen outside the
hotel. Everything, every piece of equipment gone. Lenny's

*Palladium, New York City, 1979*

1962 Stratocaster, vintage amplifiers, Toddy's tools, Ivan's impeccable Les Paul. I was devastated that this would happen in Chicago, the city of my birth. I made a mental inventory of what I carried in my metal suitcase. Fred's vest and ragged tee shirt, my *Horses* jacket with its small gold horse on the lapel. Toddy's piece of ragged red silk that served as my blindfold. Robert's cross, unpublished poems, my signed copy of the Ace paperback *Junkie,* and my battered copy of *Illuminations*. I saw it as a definite portent, always a bit superstitious I had kept these things close. Everything meaningful to me when on the road save one thing. Only weeks before I had given my original Duo-Sonic a rest. I loved that guitar just as Fred loved his Rickenbacker. Now they are together, retired they lie in state beneath my bed.

We all went our separate ways, temporarily putting aside the equipment woes. Todd and Tara were wed in a mission in San Antonio with Lenny as his best man. As I traveled with Fred in Europe it occurred to me that one of the greatest rewards of touring had been that Todd and I had both found true love.

Losing my suitcase with my work clothes, tattered and irreplaceable, was hard to reconcile. I lost contact with what to wear so just wore old dungarees and tee shirts that people threw on the stage. I was also disheartened by the loss of the souped up Duo-Sonic I had gotten when I retired my original. Andi and I had spent weeks planning and acquiring a metal pick guard, Danelectro pickups, a Bigsby bar, and a rare preamp that was installed by an eccentric genius outside of Chicago. It was the loudest guitar on the stage. An animal. I felt these losses were signs that I had perhaps run my course. I hadn't made a drawing nor written in months failing even to carry a journal in my travels. I sat and listened to *Andmoreagain* by Arthur Lee. *And I'm wrapped in my armor . . . but my things are material. And I'm lost in confusions . . . 'cause my things are material.*

I was shuttling back and forth to Detroit, each parting more wrenching. I went from job to job, city to city, absurd interview after interview and an endless tour of radio stations. I deeply cared for my city, my band and crew. But after a time, if not prudent, one reaches the point of being unrecognizable to oneself. I threw open the carpet of my life. I examined where I had tramped and what I had trampled. I reflected on where I had tripped up, was unkind demanding and dismissive to others. What I had wrongly coveted and what I had tossed aside. Where I was standing and where I was destined to go. It was time to hold myself accountable trusting there was no harsher judge nor jury.

Throughout Europe, I felt overwhelmed by a frenetic wave of adoration, kids clamoring for attention and locks of my hair. Boys offered their girlfriends. Girls shed their sweaters. I never had bodyguards, and I raced down the streets of Cannes, of Bologna and Florence with fans and paparazzi at my heels. I felt they'd devour me, like the youths on the beach in *Suddenly Last Summer.* The poet Gregory Corso joined our caravan. We went to a tailor in Bologna, and I happily granted his wish for a white linen suit. Later, as he ordered an espresso in an outdoor café, dressed in white reciting Shelley, I remembered him

by the Chelsea reading my poems and nodding out with cigarette ash flecking his trousers. On the bus ride from Bologna to
Florence, several women blocked the road forcing our bus to a
halt, crying out my name. Gregory and I disembarked. Some
of the women kissed the hem of my black dress. I was horrified
as they wrung their hands and cried out to me in Italian. What
do they want? I called out in desperation. Gregory spoke flu-
ent Italian and translated for me. They want you to free their
husbands, all political prisoners, he said. They believe you have
the power to do that.

I felt like a fraud. In that moment, I knew nothing of what
they were going through, nor how to remedy it. There was a
lot I had to learn about in our world and my place within it.
Gregory took down the names of their husbands and suggested I read them out at a scheduled press conference. I agreed
to do it but felt completely ineffectual. I was just the leader of
a rock band, with no conscious political powers. I climbed back
in the bus and returned to my seat, despondent and inextrica-
bly changed.

Our last performance took place in a soccer arena in
Florence, Italy, on September 17, 1979, before eighty thousand
people, with Gregory Corso one of our greatest living poets in
the wings. Todd had wanted to raise an immense American
flag from his Navy years. It was not a political statement but a
salute to America's gift to culture: rock n roll. He told me he
was warned it may cause problems, but he wanted to raise it
one last time. I gave him the nod and he shouted to the crew,
Okay let's raise it, let's raise hell. In the end, that's what we did,
an entire season in hell in two hours.

I had forgotten my white shirt and tie at the hotel. I just went barefoot with my pants rolled up and a loose-fitting striped boatneck shirt. My brother solemnly handed me my electric guitar and I offered up one last deafening feedback out of Fred's excruciatingly loud souped-up Fender Twin. Engaging within a ring of power, I then surrendered our stage to the people, encouraging them to take over, to forget about us and become themselves. Our soundman Carl Cornell told me that from his vantage point was a sight he would never forget. What did you see, I asked. The kids, thousands of them, he sputtered, rushing forward and ascending the stage in waves.

The seal of my silent vow was cracking. It would be the second time in life that something precious had to be forsaken so that I could continue to grow. I had once cast off my religion, gave up a child. Casting off the mantle of fame and fortune seemed nothing compared to that. No one knew these thoughts, save my brother, who would bear the greatest amount of pain for my departure. He saw it in my eyes. I sensed his tears not shed.

That night Gregory and I walked the streets of Florence. He begged me not to quit. What will you do? he shouted. We stood beneath the immense statue of David. Gregory wept, but I did not comfort him. To make such a decision I needed to remain steely. I felt the needs of my people, and the loyalty and complex ambitions of my band members. *Dancing Barefoot* took on its meaning in real time, all three levels simultaneously. I knew my decision would cause pain and resentment, but I felt it necessary to reclaim who I was. When we completed *Horses,* I thought I had done my job. But encouraged and inspired by others, I stayed on with my band and we offered up a small and hopefully meaningful body of work. We had fought the good fight, and I had, in the words of Timothy, finished my course. Todd had lowered, bundled and tied the ropes around his flag, never to be raised again, and brought it to me.

Before returning to Detroit, I stopped in New York and went to see William Burroughs. He sat quietly, with his hands folded, as I told him what I had done and where I was going. Afterwards, he simply asked, What does he have to offer you? Himself, I answered. I said farewell to William, who had counseled me seven years before to keep my name clean. I had pursued the unbidden; it was the hour of pursuing my own. Rock n roll gave me the landscape to acknowledge yet renounce our musical and spiritual heritage. With an old plaid suitcase covered in stickers I returned to Detroit. I did it for love. I did it for art. But moreover, I did it for myself. It was time to cast off my old coat. The rebel hump shuddered. Walking away was my second declaration of existence.

# My Madrigal

W<small>E LIVED IN</small> every time zone, sometimes ending or beginning the night at dawn, taking up residence in the Arcade bar beneath a huge round clock with no hands. That inanimate object became our early spirit animal. Fred wrote a song about that clock, slow singing over a quick but broken beat. We moved into the Cadillac hotel full-time with a special tenancy rate. There were only a handful of occupants at the hotel.

Though somewhat isolated, I embraced Detroit fully as my new home. If Fred was at rehearsal, or running some errand, I would venture out and walk through the empty downtown streets, dressed in my old finery. A long fur military coat with lost buttons. Worn boots. Boatneck shirt. All somehow out of place, as if I was cut out of an old magazine, a bohemian paper doll walking upright, no one around. I could exist for hours, even entire days, enveloped in silence.

I loved the hotel architecture, but the interior had no aesthetically redeeming qualities. There was nothing romantic about it. Our room was small, with one orange wall, orange and black bedding and bad abstract art. A small closet and bathroom. Whatever time we rose, we had steak and eggs, and oranges, sometimes our sole sustenance. It took me a while to adjust to his slow-moving, reflective ways that contrasted with his tricky beats and blistering guitar solos.

When left to my own devices, I'd go down to the ninth floor, which was entirely empty, and enter unlocked rooms and look out the windows onto various views of the city. When I was restless, pretending to be Nijinsky, I would happily leap through the long empty hallways. I played my clarinet I had obtained in a pawn shop in Vienna, for Fred suggested I learn to play one to help strengthen my breathing and have a positive impact on my singing. He taught me some rudimentary skills and gifted me with a mouthpiece. I grew accustomed to it, I never learned to play in a traditional way but could endlessly improvise. On the road I had practiced in motel rooms, fields, public bathrooms. I never learned scales or notes; I played in my own way, which resonated an Arabian night more than the mathematics of music. I had played clarinet for William Burroughs till three in the morning at the American Hotel in Amsterdam. He understood me and when I stopped, a bit embarrassed, he motioned me to continue. That night enshrined with his loving encouragement stays within me, even now.

The hotel was planning to close for a long, involved renovation as the number of rooms was deemed impractical and far too small by contemporary standards. Finally, the owners announced that the hotel would close due to declining occupancy, which made us laugh as we were among the last of the stronghold. In those last weeks, I could play my clarinet or leap through the hallways of any floor I liked.

In 1979, it wasn't easy to find an apartment in downtown Detroit, Fred's beloved and beleaguered city. We finally located a place to live less than a mile from the hotel on East Jefferson in a dilapidated converted mansion. It had an upright piano in the entrance hall and was adjacent to the Eight O'clock Diner, open twenty-four hours, so coffee was readily available. There were two sparsely furnished apartments. One was sunny with a window overlooking a wide alley with trees. I was charmed by the chirping birds, but Fred preferred the second one. The black linoleum on the kitchen floor had five large yellow spots, invoking the Five Spot, the historic jazz club in the East Village. It was due to that floor that Fred convinced me, and we thought it a good omen.

My brother gathered my important belongings in a truck and drove from New York to Detroit. My desk, my books and notebooks, precious talismans, but much was left behind and destined for other hands. I was inspired to make my mark on our little apartment. We set up our stands for his saxophone and my clarinet. No TV but a stereo, our records, from opera to Motown to the Ray Conniff Singers to Sun Ra and John Coltrane. I hung my old Moroccan silks and wide paisley scarves over the windows. Fred found a print of a favorite Mondrian and tacked it on the wall by our instruments. We kept it sparse, everything reflected our state of mind, the artists we liked, the books we were reading. My tarot cards. Fred's motorcycle jacket. His cowboy boots taped up with black duct tape. Our five-spot floor. That is what I remember.

*East Jefferson, Detroit*

At night we would listen to our records, often ending with *A Love Supreme.* Fred's admiration for Coltrane was deep, and we listened to his records over and over, so inspired that we would improvise in the empty hallway, Fred on piano me on clarinet. We improvised long pieces that we'd repeat and perfect—*Methadone Waiting Room,* for its slow monotonous groove and another we called *Dromedaries,* because it seemed to catch the movement of camels laboring across the desert. Another for the poet Rumi, re-creating in repetitious play the whirling of the Dervishes, the turn of the skirts of the Sufi. We composed pieces that no one heard, save the spirit of the hallway, or the ghosts that might be hanging about in our little jazz apartment. We'd choose a painting from our Jackson Pollock books and interpret it; unfettered cries for the chaos of the world, improvising until the wails ascended then wound down, surrendering to the softness of sleep.

The desire for illumination eclipsed that of ambition. It seemed to some, possibly because I was no longer in the public eye, that I was doing nothing. But for our part we were mutually evolving. At first, I suffered the growing pains of an emerging moth, trying to stretch, expand, or the foal attempting to rise on uncertain limbs.

It was in this apartment that we celebrated the end of the seventies, and Fred, at the last moment of the decade, asked me to be his wife. Though already wed in my mind, it was still a challenging time when I thought I might flee, not go home, but somewhere far. Say the roof of the world, or a monastery carved on the side of a cliff overlooking the sea. Fred sensed my agitation, my longing for the sea, and took my hand, and gave me ground. He had bought a dark brown 1973 Oldsmobile at a used car lot and we drove all the way to the Upper Peninsula. Grand Sable Dunes were left by enormous glaciers, massive dunes nestled along the shore with the pounding waves of Lake Michigan at our feet. I was ecstatic, embracing the dunes as desert, the lake as the sea. *Whenever you miss the ocean,* he said, *I will bring you here.*

When I wrote my parents that we planned to marry, my father wrote that he would like to visit us alone. I was somewhat anxious yet honored for my father never traveled. He wanted to see what kind of life I was living, inspect my husband to be, and sense why I left public life. Perhaps to reassure my mother, who was heartbroken that I left such golden opportunities behind. Fred picked him up at the airport; he arrived in his best clothes and a new overcoat. They took to each other immediately. Both were mutually respectful, soft-spoken, dignified. Fred took my father to the Hotel Saint Regis with its classic bar, and the two sipped cognac and talked for hours. It was the first time my father showed real interest in my choice of fellows. He was impressed with Fred's potential athleticism, his coolness and sense of humor and his knowledge of sports and politics. They returned in high spirits.

My father was a fine golfer, and he had convinced Fred to allow him to instruct and guide him. We soon arranged to travel to South Jersey to meet my family and have his first lesson. My father was astonished by Fred's prowess and how swiftly he took to the game. Both had a sense of the importance of form, of the beauty inherent in golf, as much a mental game as physical. In the evenings, Fred would sit with my mother at the kitchen table, smoking cigarettes, talking about life. Both were excellent listeners, my mother a stellar storyteller. I was content to leave him alone with them, happy that Fred was taken with them and they with him.

It was a leap year when Fred and I were married. We exchanged vows at the Mariners' Church in downtown Detroit, where sailors were blessed before putting out to sea. The night before, on February 29th the moon was all but full, with what looked like two bright lights hanging close. They are planets, he said. They are us, I was thinking. In the morning, I made breakfast and dressed quickly. I wore a white Victorian tea dress and white tights. It never occurred to me to buy white shoes; I was oblivious to this misstep but still recall that my black ballet flats seemed to disturb my new mother-in-law. Fred, handsome as always, wore a black suit, white cuffed shirt, and black silk tie. We drove a few blocks on East Jefferson to the church. The Lafayette Coney Island where we met, the Renaissance hotel where we first kissed, the Cadillac hotel where we first lived together, and our apartment were minutes from one another. The five points of our wayward yet steadfast star.

Ours was a modest wedding, only our parents were present. My father in his dress suit and calm demeanor quietly reigned. My mother chain-smoked. Fred's father paced. His mother, in a pristine pink suit, was a bundle of nerves. Father Ingles wore a heavy gold anchor in place of a crucifix. I had chosen white chrysanthemums. Fred had selected the organ music, *Jesu, Joy of Man's Desiring* by J. S. Bach, Charles-Marie Widor's *Toccata, Abide with Me,* and the hymn *O Come, O Come, Emmanuel,* that he knew I loved.

*March 1st, 1980, Mariners' Church*

The ceremony was light but solemn. We knelt before Father Ingles, received his blessings. Going through the Scriptures, we had chosen the counsel from Hebrews 13:16, which my father read in his sonorous voice. *But to do good and to communicate forget not: for with such sacrifice God is well pleased.* We rose and exchanged rings. Mine was a simple gold band, a bit loose, so Fred wrapped it with black string. His was an antique gold band with FREDERICK engraved inside, that I had bought for him, with secret hopes, sometime before at the Portobello Market in London.

My mother and father gifted us with a large white goblet, like a souvenir of Camelot. When we returned to the apartment, I heated us Campbell's New England chowder which we shared from the goblet. We had to hurry to the airport and nearly missed our flight to Miami. I had an old camel's hair coat that I threw over my wedding dress. I ran ahead to assure they wouldn't close the doors of the plane. Fred did not run, he shuffled. The stewardess called for him to hurry, but he went his pace.

The flight was crowded. At mid-flight there was a terrible storm. Lightning struck the windows. The turbulence was harrowing, people were screaming. Fred had a small bottle of cognac my father had given us, and we sat quietly, exchanging sips. He took my hand and said, If we go down, we'll go together. I loved him, but I knew we would prevail. The man behind us was shouting we're going to die over and over, and his son started crying. I stood up, held on to the seat and turned to face him, announcing loudly that nothing was going to happen to us, that we had just gotten married and were on our honeymoon and not to fear as this was merely part of the adventure. People fell silent. Beyond us was the full moon in Virgo, Fred's sign. We had hoped to view the lunar eclipse later that night if things had turned out as planned. Beneath us somewhere the tides were high, and the sea was churning. We finally landed in Fort Lauderdale to refuel. Very few of us agreed to get back on the plane. We landed in Miami at midnight almost seven hours later than expected.

We had two small suitcases. Fred got a car from an all-night rental, and we headed out without a plan or reservation. We drove beneath the full moon, passing one no-vacancy sign after another. About two in the morning, I spotted a vacancy sign with an arrow. We drove off the highway onto a dirt road, a long one leading to a small office across a one-story motel like in *Psycho,* whitewashed with a hand-painted sign: NIRVANA MOTEL. Fred woke the proprietor who wasn't very happy but perhaps seeing us standing there with our two small suitcases and me in the moonlight in my limp Victorian gown gave him pause. He gave Fred a key and we walked to the edge of the nearby shore. We looked up at the triangular curve of our moon, Jupiter, and Mars. My ballet shoes were full of sand, and I washed my feet in the sea. Our room was modest, the mattress close to the floor. I took off my dress, and we spent our first night as man and wife.

Perhaps it was the planets and the moon and the power of love that protected me, for my armor seemed impenetrable. I had sensed no danger, I knew we'd prevail, just as I knew when we waltzed in the center of that highway in Detroit. And that feeling I had experienced on the plane stayed with me at dawn when we sped across the seven-mile bridge at 140 miles an hour toward the Florida Keys. Suddenly a tire blew, and Fred held the wheel through a tremendous skid, expertly executed a spin and halt. He got out and inspected the tire; he was quietly pleased at my reaction. Are you okay? Yes, I said, I had no doubt you would handle it. Fred walked the bridge, found an emergency call booth, told the rental agency that we blew a tire, that it was harrowing, we were fine, but needed a replacement as we were on our honeymoon. After a time, they apologetically brought us a sporty red convertible, an upgrade. Tell me the truth, he asked, were you frightened? No, I said, I never learned to drive, I leave that to you, but I think you could have been a great stock car racer. I'm your racer, he said.

When we finally pulled into the Keys the first thing Fred did was take me to a jewelry store and buy a ring guard for my wedding ring. He placed the black thread, a sacred remnant, in a tiny compartment in his wallet. We visited Ernest Hemingway's home where Fred took a photograph of me in a white room flooded with light standing next to an antique birthing chair, an unprofessed sign of things to come.

Our lease for the apartment would be up in a few months so we searched everywhere for a new home. By chance we turned on a small dead-end street while off exploring side streets in St. Clair Shores, where there was a hidden system of canals. By accident we found what appeared the perfect place, a vine-covered stone house, built at the turn of the century that resembled a Belgian country house. It was a miniature version of my first castle that I gazed at as a toddler from the stoop on Baring Street. A quiet echo of the sprawling mansions Linda and I walked past on the way to school. Someday I will live in a house like that I had told her, though later in life I had no such ambition, happy with an East Village sixth-floor walkup. Yet something stirred within me, when we drove past it that winter afternoon, searching for our own place. It wasn't for sale, yet I had a premonition that we would one day live there.

The thought of living on a canal intrigued us. On Klenk Island on the far east side of Detroit we found a plot of land on a canal just a short boat ride to the mouth of the Detroit River. Fred had the idea to build a small house there and we made plans through the nights. But after weeks of negotiating the deal fell through. In a way I felt secretly relieved, thinking of the house on Beach Street. Whenever we went on a drive, we'd somehow wind up back to that dead-end street, tree-lined with no sidewalks, ending on the entrance to Lake St. Clair. We'd park there unnoticed and imagine the future.

We found a little house on Olive Street near a train line. We sat in the car as trains went by, somewhat mournfully, try-ing to imagine living there. On Good Friday we took a long drive and turned down Beach Street just to see the house one more time before making our offer. Our small but fervent prayer was answered. There, in the front yard, was a for sale by owner sign nailed to a post on the front lawn. The owners proved difficult to work with, but we finally came to terms and were set to move in on the first of April. But the end of May arrived, and they showed no sign of leaving. Fred had a few altercations with them, they begrudgingly agreed to be out by the first of July. On July 2nd we pulled up to our new home to find the front yard piled with trash and the house filled with debris. For two days from morning through twilight we cleared as much as possible. Exhausted, we slept on our coats spread over a mattress.

We woke up and it was Independence Day. There was much to be done, and we christened this period as our summer of manual labor. There was a spiral staircase leading to three rooms upstairs and a small bathroom. Our room had a wrought iron balcony covered in wild roses. Ivy covered the entire house. There were huge mounds of dirt that we returned to the pit the former owners had dug to install an unfinished swimming pool. I uncovered an old stone bench beneath where eventually our children would sit in years to come. All these discoveries were a delight; even with all the work needed, it was for us a romantic house.

It touched me deeply to have our own trees to shepherd. High ancient willows lined the canal. In the back, beyond the kitchen, a boathouse filled with sandbags, mops, and sump pumps running as it was constantly flooded. I realized I had little sense of how to set up a house. Everywhere I had lived was makeshift. Using whatever someone else left behind, adding one's own, then leaving most behind and starting over. Slowly we set up house. I knew how to cook and do laundry from helping my mother. And Fred took over setting up furniture. The former owner had painted all the walls red and Fred had to get a huge ladder to repaint the high walls.

I wanted a used piano to improvise on, as we had in the hall of our apartment. We found an old Chickering, and it became the centerpiece of our music room, joining a small TV on a cloth-covered trunk, stands for my clarinet, his sax and acoustic guitar. My Georgian-style desk that Todd had brought from New York no longer suited me. It became Fred's office desk, with a clock, a picture of his mother as a child, and our first telephone and answering machine.

My favorite room was the kitchen. It was small, but big enough for a card table by the screen door becoming my own café. I made my coffee and sat and wrote anytime beguiled by the ivy, the willows, the turret, the screen door at the side of the house. We knew it was impractical with only one small bathroom upstairs. Not much closet space and no washer or dryer. Things I never thought about before. With the lake only steps away, I entered a life that was not monastic, save by my own design. Ideas came and went. If one fell through another descended upon us, like a small craft, a single engine plane, dropping a handful of leaflets. Next move. Next course of study. The winters were cold, dark. The canal froze. There was nothing luxurious about it, yet entirely romantic, uniquely ours, and with each spring the scent of lilacs and roses, cooing doves and in autumn, pears falling at my feet.

Before our children were born, I created a room of my own. It was adjacent to our bedroom, small, square-shaped with one window. I had a vision of how it should serve me inspired by *One Thousand and One Nights*. Fred had found a surplus store where we bought long wide rolls of black felt, a small hammer, boxes of nails, and two-sided black electrical tape. I worked on my own, unrolling the felt, covering and framing the entire floor. The wall was white plaster, with one window overlooking our wild yard overgrown with lilac bushes.

At a secondhand store I found a low table, and I covered a wide throw pillow with heavy Moroccan striped silk. I prepared fresh mint tea, drank from my Persian cup, sat with my inkwell and fountain pen to write. I felt I had captured exactly as I had read, a mysterious room in the *Arabian Nights* for tea and rumination. In this room I felt entirely myself. There I could sit and write in the morning light, or at night by candlelight. Sometimes I would not lift my pen, but my mind would conjure long stories that seemed to come from another source, fluid and continuous when I'd leave to prepare a meal or fold our clothes. The room was my *vagabondia*. Fred would sometimes stop and look inside but never entered it. Not once did he disturb the atmosphere, or tread upon the black felt with his dusty cowboy boots.

Soon after we were married, Fred expressed the wish for a son. I hadn't thought of having children, expecting us to live a kind of rootless bohemian life. He promised first to take me anywhere in the world. I chose Saint-Laurent-du-Maroni, a border town in Northwest French Guiana. We planned the complicated journey, drawing out maps, centering our goals. He read history. I read *The Thief's Journal*.

The following February, we flew to Miami, connecting to Guadalupe, Haiti, then Surinam. From a dock in Paramaribo, Fred hired two young men in a wood pirogue to row us across the piranha-infested Maroni River. They dropped us off on the opposite shore in torrential rain. With much effort we climbed a steep embankment, following a path to the town of Saint-Laurent, where chained convicts were once paraded in the streets. We found a local bar and drank coffee laced with

*Prison, Saint-Laurent-du-Maroni*

cognac waiting for the rain to end. Not far was the modest Hotel Galibi, perfectly located in the center of nowhere.

On Valentine's Day, I stood before the mass cell of the abandoned Saint-Laurent prison, formerly inhabited by coarsened guards and hardened criminals. This had been my goal, to be at the exact spot that Jean Genet had rhapsodized. It struck me that it could be a long time before we'd be free to tackle another such quest. Herein I would venture in my mind, as I did with my siblings, playing the game of knobs, carried away to Neverland or the rings of Saturn. Lost in these thoughts, I was unaware that Fred took my photograph. In this simple image I can quietly relive the interior arc of that moment. Entering the mass cell, I knelt and chose three stones from the dirt floor and placed them in an oversized Gitanes matchbox.

Fred and I celebrated our first anniversary in Kourou. It was a bright Sunday afternoon. Unable to book passage to Devil's Island, we sat on a bench holding hands and watched as the boat departed to the site of the penal colony where Alfred Dreyfus was incarcerated, and Papillon planned his miraculous escape.

Upon our return, we continued our travels through our books. At night Fred would read of sea voyages or consult his nautical maps. At the same time, I was writing an imaginary journal of a traveler who never traveled, only through the seven league boots of his mind that transported him to Damascus, remote monasteries, and the deserts of Arabia. Fred found a book of aerial views of Cairo for me, and I found some obscure yellowed journals of unknown seamen for him. He admired the great captains in history and literature. When we drove east to see my family, we would stop at coastal towns in New England to visit historical museums and the sites of Yankee whaling vessels. I had little affinity with ships, save the imagined wooden boats of Neverland. But he loved them and hoped to one day own an old Chris-Craft to sail Lake St. Clair.

At night, Fred read of Silas Talbot who rose from farm boy to captain of Old Ironsides, and Jacob Le Maire, a Dutchman who was the first to sail around Cape Horn. But most of all, he revered Captain Joshua Slocum. Nova Scotia born, Slocum was trained to be a shoemaker but yearned for the sea. Obstinate and driven, he ran away at fourteen to be a cabin boy, and at sixteen he signed on as an ordinary seaman on a merchant ship. Despite that he couldn't swim, he was the first man to single-handedly circumnavigate the earth before his disappearance at sea. Fred would read long passages aloud of Slocum's account beginning with the immortal words: *I had resolved on a voyage around the world.* Fred considered going down to Argentina to see the Cape himself. Because I couldn't swim, the idea of long journeys in the cabin of a sailing vessel wasn't appealing. I imagined going along to see the sheep on the Falkland Islands and once again I found a way to join him, my Captain. And what is a Captain but the commander of a good ship, to look up to, learn from and be protected by.

At winter's end, we took long drives searching for an old Chris-Craft. I would explore the boatyards drawn to old tugboats, makeshift vessels, hideouts of hobos and squatters. One day, in a town called Harrison, about fourteen miles from our house, I saw a boat that stole my heart. A small wooden vessel like in *Wynken, Blynken, and Nod*. Big enough for two people, hand-carved with a glowing patina and one blue sail. It wasn't at all practical, and somewhat overpriced, but I easily pictured sailing up and down our canal. Fred knew I loved it, and we stood and admired it together until I was ready to leave. If I seemed glum, he'd get in the truck, and we'd ride up to Harrison to visit the boat lot. I had a little song . . . *Sail little boat sail on / Dear little boat be true / We always hoped for one little boat like you.*

One afternoon Fred said he had some business in Ann Arbor and left in his truck. I wasn't privy to what transpired, but when he got home, he seemed melancholy. We sat at the table, and he confessed, that with an advance for future work he drove to Harrison to buy the boat for me, but it was gone. We commiserated in silence. I was very moved that he would do that, and the little boat remained in the treasury of our memory, like a lost child. I can still picture it, a boat big enough for two with one blue sail, the only boat I ever wished for, the one that would find its way into poems, stories, my hazy waterways. Weeks later, Fred surprised me with an even more precious gift, an Abyssinian kitten, a ruddy with gold eyes, predicting she would be a great huntress. She was lively and graceful, so we called her Ballo, which in Latin means to dance and leap about. We had been plagued with mice, and she lived up to Fred's assessment. She had a mystical aspect, and I felt at one with her.

In time Fred found our boat, in Saginaw, Michigan. A retired seaman who was quite fond of drink sold it to Fred for a very low price. It was a thirty-foot 1957 Chris-Craft Constellation, a bit woebegone but still beautiful. Fred and a buddy hauled it back to St. Clair Shores on a trailer. It

Nawadir

*Our Captain*

took several hours because they had to drive very slowly. He was home by nightfall. The boat took up quite a bit of our yard. Curious neighbors gathered; Ballo found a new hiding place.

That first morning, after breakfast, we immediately began cleaning, sanding, painting, and creating her waterline. I knew nothing of boats but worked diligently. I was unprepared and ill-suited for the tasks at hand; my mother's voice hovered, admonishing me for making so little progress drying dishes and other chores. I was never able to muster the specific kind of energy required to finish my duties quickly and efficiently. At thirty-three, I mused, I am in so many ways the same twelve-year-old girl.

That spring, the lilacs bloomed, the long-haired branches of our ancient willows swayed. The interior of the boat suited us. It had a jazz feeling, with its speckled Formica table. We'd sit there and inventory the things we still needed to buy: a ship's compass, life jackets, and material for curtains that I would sew by hand. In the evenings we'd sit in the boat with a thermos of coffee for me and a Budweiser for Fred, listening to Tiger baseball on the transistor radio. Fred would spread out his nautical maps, studying Lake St. Clair, and the best route in going across the Detroit River to Ontario. He studied course plotting, compass reading, steering, navigational routes. I would read about Egypt, Thebes, and the Sahara, and we'd often laugh, as it was not lost on either of us that our Formica table was divided between the sea and the desert.

In late summer we christened her *Nawadir,* Arabic for rare and precious thing, from Gérard de Nerval's *The Women of*

*Cairo*. Fred scheduled a boat inspection; her wood gleaming, her name shining in the sun. The admiring neighborhood kids gathered around the front of the house to watch when it would be hauled to the marina and put out into the water. The inspector took a long time and asked to see Fred privately. It turned out that our trailer had a broken axle and could not be moved, but there were also other costly inherent problems that would have to be addressed to make her seaworthy. Fred took it well, but *Nawadir* was grounded and stayed moored in our yard, reverberating with the sounds of baseball and Beethoven, never to touch the sea.

There were record low temperatures in January 1982. Deciding to escape the below freezing weather and head south, we packed Fred's guitar, some clothes and books and drove through Cincinnati, Kentucky, Georgia through the Okefenokee Swamp to Jacksonville, Florida. One motel blurred with another. A yellow light bulb that intermittently flickered and then it began to rain. A motel room where everything worked with quarters, like sleeping in the Laundromat. Feeding quarters in the TV, the ice machine, the vibrating bed. There was a white dresser with a starched doily and an empty glass vase of artificial flowers that I mistakenly watered.

We were entranced by Amelia Island. The coastline was anchored by the canals and bays, shrimp trawlers, rusty tugs, and refurbished fishing boats. Fred was interested in how the people conducted their lives and wondered if we too could live on a small houseboat in winter. On Valentine's Day we went horseback riding on the beach. I had a white horse and Fred's was a speckled grey. It was the only time I ever saw him ride. His horse broke in a run, and I followed. Had it been a scene in a movie, I could have happily made it never ending.

On the way to Saint Augustine, we stumbled upon American Beach, seemingly forgotten. It was our kind of place, where one could hide out in the open. We stood on a sloping dune looking out at the ruins of a once great dance hall, where jazz had flourished, exuberant, free of boundaries. In the late hours, it was like a Christmas truce in the Civil War. Feasting and dancing, all united by the cry of the saxophone rising and spilling into the sea.

In Saint Augustine, we happened upon a red and white striped lighthouse, overlooking the bay. It was for sale, easily fitted for living. It was affordable and had been empty for some time. Newly inspired, we decided to buy it and live there in the winter months. Fred could study the sea, and I could write. We were about to close when the local government stepped in, declaring the lighthouse a historical site, and the deal fell through. In those last days on the beach, I was sure I was carrying our child. We headed back home and confirmed what I already suspected, leaving behind the sea, thoughts of tugboats and shrimp trawlers, and the lighthouse at lookout point. We stopped once more at American Beach. It was rather chilly, and I was wearing a thick white sweater. Fred regarded all before him as if it was his fallen kingdom of abandoned structures and grassy dunes.

–It's a J. G. Ballard world now, he said.

There were stretches of silence during the long drive home. A comfortable, trusting silence as each of us considered the changes sure to come. I never imagined myself with children. I never imagined living a long life. I just hoped to live long enough to do something of merit and to find a companion to love and work with. Now, I was augmenting these hopes with thoughts of new responsibilities and the anticipation of a child on the way. I had no doubt at all that we would have the son Fred wished for.

Fred desired to compose a new kind of symphony, with movements inspired by Coltrane, Sun Ra, and above all, Beethoven. We attended the conductor Antal Dorati's cycle of the nine symphonies at the Detroit Symphony Orchestra and on rainy afternoons we listened to cassettes of the piano concertos in our boat now permanently moored in the yard. On certain stormy nights we'd listen to Symphony No. 3 *Eroica,* on our record player. The second movement, a unification of grief and ecstasy, was Fred's favorite piece of music. We'd picture Napoleon, who Beethoven once revered, rising from his camp bed, a general with no army, alone on the jagged cliffs of exile. Through the power of music, we saw the man who betrayed his anti-monarchial ideals, crowning himself Emperor, staggering along the edge of purgatory. Afterwards Fred would change the record, place the needle on the second movement of the Seventh Symphony, which I favored, hold out his arms and say, C'mon, Trisha, let's dance.

Our life was obscure, perhaps not so interesting to some, but for us it was a whole life. Sometimes challenging, yet I could feel my own evolution in slow, but real time. It was painful, as though scrubbing centuries of skin, ash, debris, from an

*St. Clair Shores, Michigan*

unearthed vessel coming at last into its own. *rebel hump rebel hump*. I am the same person, I would say to myself, only better. I grew lighter, healthier, and sure of the vocation I had chosen above all others. That of a writer.

In my longing for travel, to walk other streets in other lands, I converted small areas in my mind. The corner of the bait shop at the end of the block, with its whitewashed walls and empty lot was my Morocco. I would make mint tea and walk the short distance and sit against the wall, particularly when it was hot, and imagine myself in Tangier, where the sea meets the desert. At the other end of the block was my Marseilles. I could see the boats in the distance on Lake St. Clair. The decks were home to large cement blocks embedded with heavy brass circular hooks, once used for docking small craft. Transmogrified, these simple elements became a whole port city, the city of sailors and the dying Rimbaud.

In my room with the black felt floor was a table and my seven volumes, bound in navy silk, of Richard Burton's translations of *One Thousand and One Nights*. I no longer needed to read them, merely run my fingers over the gold cloth title on the spine, as deft fingers over braille, unleashing hopes. My mind was always active, entertaining me through the tedium of dishes to be washed, food prepared, clothes laundered. I was as slow with my chores as when young, which exasperated my mother so much, but this was my own home, and no one took me to task. I went about my domestic duties at my own pace.

I never saw the great stupa overlooking Kathmandu. I never cruised the Nile in a two-masted sailing boat. But writing of an imagined Egyptian winter, my *Thebes Journal,* was so embedded in my cells, that my season of study seemed to produce memory. The restored song of the Colossi of Memnon. Reading passages of what I had written to my sister over the phone, she seemed quite surprised. It was a story in which I had played a somnambulist in a low budget film and witnessed a murder in the shadows of the Pyramids. "You never told me you did that," she'd said, and I was satisfied, for on some level I had. Linda was my lifeline. She listened avidly to my stories and encouraged me to continue. We exchanged commentary on the books of the Bible. We read *Villette* by Charlotte Brontë discussing the world of Lucy Snowe over the phone, living within its atmosphere. Distance meant nothing to us; we seamlessly moved from world to world together.

Toward the end of my pregnancy, it was no longer possible for me to sit on the floor at my low table. Sometimes I just stood at the door and watched the light change, gazing upon the room as if it were a secret corridor of my mind. When it was time to create a space for our son, we dismantled and removed everything, rolling up the black felt. There are no existing photographs of my room, but in memory I can see it in close-up, down to the small fibrous hairs of black felt, catching the dust that filled the shafts of light from the window. It inspired many mental adventures, and eventually it was transformed into a cheery though humble playroom. In the years to come, I would peek in and watch Jackson play with his soldiers and robots and dinosaurs. He would sit on the floor, just as I had, creating worlds of his own in perfect silence. Lining up his soldiers on the windowsill, not for battle but to look up at the night sky, then gather them in a small pouch before bed.

The clock never measured how we conducted our lives, but now I had to follow a child's needs, and for the first time Fred and I existed somewhat out of sync. My time was more regimented, and I developed a new work ethic. I would rise around 5 a.m., go downstairs, make some coffee, and sit at the card table. At first, I would remain in a stupor. With the arrival of dawn, I would step outside as the flowers opened, the doves cooed, and the long-haired willows swayed slightly over the dark canal. I was enthralled by small things, the wonder that our tree grew pears that fell by my feet, that wild roses climbed up the trellis, entwining our balcony, that the same doves returned every spring to nest upon it, and that the morning glory seeds I planted covered the cyclone fence at the edge of our property, bloomed an impossible blue. I loved hanging my laundry to dry on the line as my mother did, and later removing the clothespins and the diapers and the sheets that had dried in the sun. I loved the changing seasons, the quiet winter snow. On my thirty-sixth birthday there was a full lunar eclipse. Fred was sleeping with Jackson beside him in his bassinet. I wrapped Fred's winter coat around me and Ballo followed as I went up the small stone stairwell that led to the flat roof of our vacant boathouse. As I watched the eclipse, I felt optimistic about the future. Our baby son was healthy, Fred was reading books on the history of aviation, and I was working on a suite of stories I had mapped out in French Guiana. I believed the eclipse falling on my birthday to be a good omen, and we entered a period of relative peace.

I came to love those early mornings when our little son slept. This was my writing time. After a few months, it felt more natural; and I was happily awakened by my internal clock. At dawn, Jackson's breath synchronized with the breath of his father, the house was enveloped in a cocoon of sleep. I would slip downstairs and continue to pen adventures of the traveler who did not travel.

Early one morning there was a tapping at the kitchen door, I opened it and Ballo shook something from her clenched jaws. The head of a blue jay rolled across the floor; the same jay that threatened the eggs of the doves on our balcony. Ballo had given me a gift, but the sight of it troubled me, a bewildering augury. Not long after the entire sky turned a pale chartreuse; I had never witnessed such a phenomenon, and I felt conflicted by the ominous beauty. Fred said it was tornado weather. No tornado touched down, but dry lightning manifested and struck our oldest willow. I watched from our balcony horrified as it cracked and fell across the yard. The neighbors, curious and sad, stood around it. Seeing it lying there like a fallen giant caused me to shudder. I mourned it, gazing at the wide gap on the canal where it once acted as a veil and seemed to protect our womb of a world.

Fred finished *The Spirit of St. Louis,* the autobiography of Charles Lindbergh, and announced he wanted to learn to fly. He hadn't finished high school, and with a breathtaking diligence, completed his education and then aced classes in higher mathematics, everything required of a future pilot. In February 1985 we embarked on a new adventure. We first drove to Kill Devil Hills to pay homage to the Wright Brothers, then continued with our two-and-a-half-year-old son back to Saint Augustine. We got an inexpensive motel room with a

kitchenette by the beach. Fred attended flight school. I would sit on the beach with Jackson who played quietly by my side. I wrote, Fred flew, and I felt like I could live like that forever. I was reading *Queer,* sent to me by William. His new introduction, a writer's confession, filled me with the excited disquiet one feels upon taking a vow. I knew then with all my being that to be a writer was what I wanted more than anything.

Back home in Michigan the card table by the screen door in the kitchen became my permanent writing desk. I had tacked a postcard picture of Albert Camus to the wall. It was there for so long that our son thought it was his uncle, and he made a green glazed frame for it with the teeth of a robot. I once desired a fine desk, with secret compartments and the glowing patina of time. Yet it was at that small folding table where I cherished a sacred process, where I felt I could call myself a writer. Yet on some occasions nothing came, as if overnight everything went dry. When prolonged, these were the most difficult of times, when imagination turned on itself and even nature, with its prevailing innocence, failed to move me. My empty journal aside, I would reluctantly rise from my table to make breakfast, and Jackson and I would take a walk to the end of the street that abutted with Lake St. Clair. We'd sit on the cement barriers and look out toward Ontario. And then unexpectedly I would glimpse it, far off in the distance, my rebel hump, slowly heading for parts unknown without me, producing a sensation akin to fainting, so deep within that nothing else seems to exist save longing. Then Jackson's small hand would grip mine. Time to go, he'd say, and we'd walk back home, past the small plaster deer nestled among the chicory and pine. Then letting go, he'd race ahead to greet his father standing at the screen door.

–Where you been? Fred would ask.

Parts unknown, I'd be thinking.

–Just to the end of the block, our boy said hello to the deer.

Fred always knew when I was somewhere else; perhaps he imagined I was back on the road with my band or roaming the boulevards of Paris. But I was not there at all, nor among my memories. I was far beyond, following that shape, that triangular outline that intermittently though faithfully calls for me. The breath circulating in my nostrils was the breath of dragons, those conceived by children, and my heart was a known thing. I held the shape of things that did not come unless I bid them, characters in stories reluctant to be born, until I shook the cage of imagination, shocked them free to wreak havoc, gather wishes and trample time.

There was a sudden rainstorm. I went out to get the clothes off the line and Ballo sped out the door. She disappeared in the brush and would not return when I called. I slipped on my raincoat but could not find her and assumed she was in some hiding place or prowling for possums. I worried as it got dark when she failed to return, and Fred went out with a flashlight to look for her. He came back with Ballo in his arms. A neighbor saw her struck by a speeding car on our small dark street. I recalled with cruel clarity, her prowling through the grass, my sleek huntress. Extremely independent but unquestionably mine. In the morning, I wrapped my Abyssinian warrior in an Ethiopian cloth, and we buried her by the stone bench beneath the lilac trees. I hadn't given my heart to an animal companion since Bambi. The memory of my father wrapping her in a blanket and burying her by the side of the house magnified my sorrow. For a time, I felt restless and uneasy without Ballo traipsing after me, for she had entered the realm of the disappeared, the heart's private burial ground.

Fred studied the history of aviation and took his pilot lessons very seriously. He had exchanged circumnavigating the seas for sailing the skies, logging the required hours necessary to fly solo with instructors. We attended air shows in Detroit and Ohio, and he was humbled to meet the surviving Tuskegee Airmen. Fred secured his pilot's license, certified on November 30, 1985, after logging nearly ninety hours with instructor or solo. To celebrate he rented a Piper Cherokee, and we flew over Detroit. He was proud of his accomplishment, but he soon became painfully aware that the cost of renting even the smallest plane was prohibitive. Only on special occasions he would take me up and we'd fly above the shoreline and dunes of Northern Michigan.

Soon after Fred told me he would like us to have a daughter, and we quietly stored our hopes. Our lifestyle was frugal but in hoping for another child we also needed to generate more income to support a growing family. Our common interest in music had spawned many songs, so we decided to make our own record. Having Clive's blessing Fred put all he had into it, preparing to co-produce with Jimmy Iovine. In early October I fell ill. Our intuitive Lebanese doctor, Daher Rahi, did not examine me, but looked in my eyes, took my hand and said, the thing you have wished for has come true. He said it was too early to take a test, but he was sure I was pregnant.

We never anticipated the maelstrom that would quickly engulf our lives. Robert was admitted to the hospital with HIV-related pneumonia. Fred packed up the car, we left Jackson with my parents and drove to New York. Robert had been discharged and was hopeful. Together we went to the hospital to see Sam, suffering the last stages of AIDS. Sam asked me to sing to him and I chose the lullaby that Fred and I had just written for Jackson. I sang, conscious that our once healthy and vibrant friend was facing his end while I was carrying new life.

It was an unstoppable zeitgeist of emotionally challenging life events. Robert was soon diagnosed with AIDS, and we returned to New York to see him in the hospital, confident he could beat the virus. There was not much news about AIDS in Michigan, yet nearly every week, old friends appeared in the obituaries, dancers, fashion designers, museum curators. Richard Sohl would bring me news about the state of things in New York and stay with us to work on piano arrangements with Fred. Though Fred could be guarded with people, the two became quite close. At night when I turned in, Richard played piano concertos by Mendelssohn for him.

In January Sam Wagstaff died of complications due to AIDS. Robert was deeply shaken by the loss of Sam and asked me to write a poem for him to read at Sam's memorial. That night I focused on one of Sam's favorite images: Robert's stark white tulip gracefully bending against a black background. A black you can get lost in, Sam had said. Fred and I also wrote the lilting *Paths That Cross* as a song of solace for Robert and the many people who were losing their loved ones to AIDS.

Our daughter, Jesse Paris, was born in the same hospital as Jackson, greeted by a double rainbow. Fred was ecstatic, Jackson the first to hold her. My sister flew to Detroit to help me. I was exhausted, and she tended to me. She gave Jesse her first bath, sang to her as she carried her from room to room when she cried, until I was strong enough to do it myself. Our little silent nurse had grown, with a daughter of her own, she had fully embraced her faith and was on her own journey. Yet we were always us, nothing had changed nor altered in time. The same unshakeable love and loyalty created an aura about us.

*Dream of Life* was delayed due to the births of three girls, Jimmy Iovine and our engineer Thom Panunzio also welcomed daughters. Inspired by the birth of Jesse we wrote the title song for her. The last song, *Looking for You,* was a bright love song to Fred and the city of Detroit. Clive was very taken with the album and telegrammed to congratulate us. But even Clive Davis could not anticipate nor shield us from the personal attacks and cruel reception it was soon to face. Nonetheless Clive had faith in *People Have the Power,* a rallying call for the future. Arista released it as a single and Robert took my photograph for the cover. Fred admired the shot but observed that Robert's pictures of me somehow seemed to resemble him. Robert smiled knowingly; I stood apart as they were talking and laughing, the love of my life and the artist of my life. The single did not garner much airplay, another terrible disappointment, especially for Fred. *People Have the Power* was Fred's concept; it had been his great hope that it would serve as a voice for the people and universally benefit those supporting righteous causes. The following months were difficult, as we processed the album's failure and facing the progression of Robert's illness.

It became increasingly difficult to speak to Robert on the phone as each call was dominated by his debilitating cough. In February we visited my family, dropped off Jack and Jesse and drove back to New York. I went to see Robert on my own, no one was there but his nurse. It was a blessed visit for he did not cough, and we had a peaceful intimate afternoon. It was unbearable to say goodbye, so I waited until he slept, but as I was leaving, I turned back to see him once more. I stood there quietly, and he opened his eyes and smiled, just as he did the first time we met. I knew then in my heart it would be the last.

When I was a senior in high school President Kennedy was assassinated. Distraught, I watched his funeral with my family and all of America on television. I was inconsolable and could not eat and fell ill at Thanksgiving dinner, fainting in my father's arms. I was admitted to the hospital and given a series of blood tests. I turned seventeen in the hospital and spent New Year's Eve alone listening to Ray Charles sing *Ol' Man River* on a transistor radio. While there, I discovered that my boyfriend had found a new girlfriend. I guess I cried but not as much as during our president's funeral. Not as much as watching John-John, on his third birthday, salute his father. Not as much as seeing Jackie Kennedy's face partially visible through a black veil. I cried for her and our country and all our youthful hopes. The doctors could not diagnose what was wrong with me, calling it a blood disorder. But I truly believed that I had grieved myself sick. With the loss of Robert, the wrenching of a part of me, I struggled not to plunge into that same abyss. On Easter break we drove to North Carolina. I sat on the beach watching Jack teach Jesse how to build a sandcastle. When the tide rolled in it swept little Jesse's castle away and I comforted her.

We returned to New York in May for Robert's memorial service. Fred wore a new suit. I was proud to introduce him, my husband, to old friends and acquaintances. Only then was I struck by the absence of so many taken by AIDS. Toward the end of the service, I sang a little song I had written for him by the sea. Afterwards I kissed his mother, and we all said our farewells. Fred and I walked hand in hand through Central

Park beneath a cloudless sky. Back in Michigan I did my best to still the pall of sorrow that had veiled our household. Lilacs and morning glories bloomed, and we were heartened by the brightness of nature permeating the dark breath of mortality. The laughter of neighborhood children filled our yard as I sat quietly in the kitchen and feverishly wrote *The Coral Sea,* a metamorphic cycle of prose poems for Robert.

Throughout the winter Fred worked on new material for another album called *Going West.* The centerpiece was to be a song he called *Gone Again.* Fred was studying the history of the Kiowa and asked me to write lyrics from a matriarch's point of view, speaking to her people of the interminable return of nature's seasons. Inspired by our progress he called Richard, and they spoke of working on the songs in future months and perhaps play a little Mendelssohn. On June 1st I was shocked to read an obituary of the painter Carl Apfelschnitt, who was once Richard's great love. Two days later a tearful Andi Ostrowe called to tell us that Richard had suffered heart failure on Fire Island. As a child, he had rheumatic fever that apparently damaged his heart valve. There were no hospitals on the island, and he was flown by helicopter to the city. Richard died in the sky in the arms of our friend Danny Fields. Fred quietly wept then went outside and sat alone by the canal. Richard was only thirty-seven years old; he had quit smoking, cropped his curls and had never seemed more alive. I remembered being in Carl's loft with Richard, dressed in black standing before Carl's life-size portrait of me. There were paint spatters on the floor, Carl's overalls, and all over his shoes.

Now they were both gone and somehow the mental image of those paint spattered shoes unleashed unstoppable tears. Tears that were also for Sam and Robert and an unknown quantity burrowing a small hole in my heart.

After we were married and for the next fourteen years, save for the handful of hours in the hospital giving birth to our son and daughter, Fred and I were never apart. We had dwelled beneath the clock with no hands, lived inside the same skin, sailed the same boat that never left the land. Jesse drew happy mice and flowers in my journals. In the evening Jackson could be found sitting by the canal with his fishing pole listening to Pavarotti on his boom box. On sleepless nights or in the early morning hours I would write. Barefoot, I would tread lightly down the marble stairs, pass through the wood door with the stained-glass image of a rising sun and step into our modest kitchen with its four-burner gas stove, a country sink, heavy oak cupboards, and my card table with an open journal and a small jar of pens. Write what cannot be written, called my meteor, my inverted sail that fell into the sea.

In the fall of 1991 Rob Tyner, the former lead singer of the MC5, died of massive heart failure. Fred, who had seemed withdrawn, remained stoic but shaken, and attended his memorial service, reading Jack Kerouac's *Safe in Heaven Dead*. Fred rarely spoke of his years with the MC5, but the death of Rob brought back the ecstatic and tragic trajectory of this momentous period of his life. He opened the battered cases of his most precious surviving guitars, a mid-sixties Mosrite with a pearl finish and his beloved 12-string Rickenbacker. He ran his fingers across their fretboards but did not play them. Both instruments possessed the aura of the cultural revolution that bands like the MC5 helped to generate.

Fred was tough yet delicate. The boxer, the revolutionary, the shortstop, the pilot. He was a troubled man, but I was never to penetrate the true nature of those troubles. He was like a man returned from the war, who never spoke of his experiences but wore it like a heavy coat in all weathers. But Fred had not been to war. The war was within himself. Fred had a difficult childhood, battled with drugs as a teenager and in his early twenties. When we met, he was only twenty-six, having put that aspect of his life aside, but his health had already deteriorated and like his beloved Coltrane and others before him, the damage was done. The trials and challenges that Fred and I suffered were our own. His decline was the tragedy of my life, and it profits no one to outline the private battles of a very private man.

In the summer of 1994 Jesse turned seven, Jackson turned twelve. We drove to Lake Ann, but we did not go out to fish. Fred was not strong enough to unmoor the boat. Instead, we sat outside in the night, holding hands, hardly speaking. When we returned, we found a letter informing us that we had paid our last mortgage payment. Our ramshackle castle was now our own. I sat outside in our yard, our little daughter, Jesse, perhaps sensing my despondency, brought me a gift. She was a rainbow and the rain, as she often cried, but her smile was the sun itself. She had plucked a dandelion; its silvery lion's head gone to seed. Make a wish, she said, blow. And there are many things I could have wished for, important, urgent things, but I wished the first thing that came to mind. That I could glide, one more time, above the grass as I did when I was her age, when I believed in everything.

In September we quietly celebrated Fred's birthday at home. We brought his beloved red Harley into the dining room where he could see it. When he slept, I sat in the kitchen writing and rewriting the same paragraphs; the light through the window of our rustic kitchen merged with the luminous flicker of a handful of words. I kept reworking a manuscript I would never finish. The tale of a traveler who did not travel, save in the mind, my sole melancholic pleasure. In autumn the pears fell to the ground, and I gathered them.

On a late October afternoon, Fred put on his overcoat. Where are you going, I wanted to ask, but I didn't. He did not take his car but walked past the whitewashed walls I called my Morocco to the fish and tackle shop. He met an old fisherman who had just caught one of the largest muskies on record. The muskie was laid out upon a tarp in the back of his pickup truck. They went across the road and had a drink together and the fisherman told him his life story. They celebrated his catch yet mourned the muskie's freedom. He is no more, the old man said to Fred.

# Mortal Shoes

SOMEWHERE WITHIN A small steamer trunk amongst precious remnants of another life is a plain grey journal containing my last writings in Michigan. I worked at the card table in the kitchen on two separate paragraphs, writing them over and over, hardly aware of the obsessive nature of my process. I did not realize they would be the last words drawn from the atmosphere that Fred and I had created. I stopped writing in late October when the weather felt ominous, as if in continuous warning of an approaching storm. The illusion of a troubled yet certain calm peeled away, and we were cruelly exposed. He was our protector, even as he struggled, the king of our woebegone castle.

When Fred went into the hospital, Linda and Toddy flew to Michigan to be with the kids. I fell asleep resting my head on the edge of his hospital bed. He had never been admitted to a hospital and believed if he ever was, he would never leave. I awoke when an orderly came in to check on him. There was a page-a-day calendar tacked to the wall, and he stopped to tear off yesterday's page. I looked up at the date and shuddered, November 4th, Robert's birthday. Fred died that afternoon, in the hospital where our children were born. Birth, love, and death, never touching, ever connected.

I laid my black pleated dress on our bed. The same I had worn when Fred and I first met, the dress Paul Getty had given me. The arc of our life in the sharp pleats of one silk garment. Long and loose fitting, fanning out when I turned. A dancer's dress, now a funeral dress. It was an overcast November morning, close friends and family gathered in Detroit's oldest cemetery beneath the statue of a benevolent angel. We buried him as our Captain, for above all he had the disposition of a Captain, even as he was bereft of a vessel.

We held a service at the Mariners' Church where Fred and I were married. His memorial corresponded with the annual ringing of twenty bells in memory of the sailors lost in the *Edmund Fitzgerald*. Father Ingles, knowing Fred's devotion to this yearly ritual, agreed to leave the flowers and the model of the fated ship on the chancel. I couldn't get up. I can't do this, I told my brother. You have to, he said, he smoothed the pleats of my dress, and we drove to the church.

–What shall I say?

–It will come to you, he said, and turned on the radio.

The song *What a Wonderful World* came on. I never liked it, but whenever Fred and I heard it, he would say, Trisha, it's your song. I would protest but he insisted it was my song. I asked Toddy why he thought Fred said that. Because you're the hopeless optimist, he said. That Fred, I thought, he's going to make me sing that darn song.

My siblings stayed with me for some days after the funeral.

Linda attended to all the domestic tasks, providing care and warmth. Toddy comforted the kids, providing a trusted sense of stability. I noticed that he had plucked his eyebrows, and his face seemed softer. Yet as always, he sat at the table, smoking a cigarette, reading the sports page. He assured me he would help raise the kids, that he would stay by my side. He promised my children he would be there for them, and we spoke of the possibility of moving to Virginia where he had a small Japanese-style home. We could all live together.

As December arrived, a feeling of hope gave me the energy I needed to shop for Christmas presents. I called for a taxi and headed out to Toys"R"Us. I returned home laden with packages, feeling a small sense of accomplishment. The answering machine was on; there were fourteen messages. We never had so many messages, and one by one, they were all the same. *Patti, call me.* Tara, my mother, my father, my sister, my sister, my sister. Toddy hadn't left me a message. I took a breath and called Linda back. What has happened to Toddy? Oh, Patti, she wept. Please don't tell me, I cried, and then the animal, which most likely dwells within us all, took over my entire body. Dropping the phone, I crouched on the ground and began to wail.

My brother suffered a massive stroke while wrapping Christmas presents for his daughter. Beside him was an open sports page and an ashtray filled with butts, but Rachael had had the last word; her hair, clothing, and makeup were perfect.

Once our childhood belonged to the three of us. As adults we'd often recount everything, our infamous pirate adventures, and our secret weapons; a slingshot, a whip of a branch

*Toddy, Austin, Texas, 1978*

or a barrette from Linda's hair, raised to the sun and transformed. Several years before he died, Toddy promised to record our stories, adding his own boyish misadventures. He assured me from time to time that he was writing them, and the book would be called *Thomas's Field*. In his small stack of diaries there was but one such story, the fall of Jackie Riley. I was moved to tears, as it spoke of my miraculous feat and his loyalty as a knight in our ingenious crusade. There, I discovered that his stories were not about a boy, but about the girl within, longing to surface. Regretfully I never got to know Rachael. I clung to the male half of my brother, so never knew him fully. But I knew his heart and can still see his pale blue eyes, feel his assuring glance.

We held the wake for Toddy in South Jersey. He was buried not far from where we were raised. I brought the Cacharel silk print dress he had once chosen for me in a shop in Cannes. It had never suited me, but he was so insistent that I purchased the dress and occasionally wore it with my motorcycle jacket. I realized sometime later that it was not a dress he imagined for me, but for Rachael. I placed it in Kimberly's hands, entrusting her to place it in the coffin to wear in his Egyptian boat toward another life.

As Christmas approached, I received a concerned call from Jimmy Iovine. Toddy had sent him a letter asking him to help me get back on my feet. Unaccustomed to writing letters, he had sent it only days before he died; I had to tell Jimmy of my brother's fate. Jimmy was heartsick and sent Jack and Jesse many gifts, took care of all our immediate needs and assured me that he was here for us always. I was grateful to Jimmy and others who offered help though at times did not have the heart to respond. For a time, I felt empty and useless. The light seemed blinding, the world demanding and harsh. I still believed I was a writer but stopped writing; the ability to translate feelings as poetry seemingly abandoned me. I no longer yearned to project myself to other distant places, the sea and the desert, and I abandoned my *Thebes Journal*. I desired nothing of the clamoring marketplaces, foreign skies, and mythic constellations. Wrapped in claustrophobic silence, I waited for some sign from Fred.

In mid-February a light snow fell, as Jack and Jesse slept, I threw on my coat to go out in the yard when the phone rang. It was Michael Stipe, calling from Spain, sheepishly confessing he was somewhat intoxicated. I didn't know Michael but loved his songs and was surprised to hear his voice. He said he was so sorry about Fred, and it occurred to him that this was most likely the first Valentine's Day I would spend without him and shyly offered to be my Valentine. This thoughtful gesture filled me with happiness that lingered throughout the lonely night.

Spring arrived, the roses bloomed early, the doves returned, building their nest as they had every spring through the past sixteen years. I could see their movements through the mosquito netting covering our bedroom window. The diffused light gave our room an otherworldly appearance. One morning I noticed Fred's Polaroid camera sitting on the shelf, along with his books on the voyages of Joshua Slocum, Donald Crowhurst, and histories of sailing vessels. I had the sudden urge to take a photograph. With the net a backdrop, I arranged a Tibetan singing bowl, then a pair of Nureyev's practice slippers. Taking these images gave me a sense of accomplishment, and through the coming months, I took several others. I could touch something I had created, unfettered by grief or joy. Those emotions were fleetingly set aside, folded like flags.

WILLIAM BURROUGHS CALLED me from his bunker, staying on the line for as long as I needed, even as I could hardly speak, conscious that I was comforted that he was on the other end. Allen Ginsberg reached out and advised me to go back to the stage, replace grief with generosity and serve the public. But I hadn't yet the will to work, drawing instead from the well of others, with nothing to give in return. Jimmy Iovine provided a respite, flying us to Malibu for a family gathering and time by the sea. At Jimmy's barbecue Bruce Springsteen expressed his condolences and was attentive to Jack and Jesse. He asked Jackson if he had ever ridden on a motorcycle. Fred had promised to take Jackson on a ride on his thirteenth birthday which was fast approaching. The next morning Bruce came to our motel door with two helmets and asked if he could take Jack for a ride. I entrusted him with my son, and they sped off into the hills on Bruce's motorcycle. They returned in a few hours shining in the unforgettable energy of a youthful escapade.

I accepted assistance so to start a new life. Eventually it was time to reenter the world, to work and repay my debts. I faltered, brushed myself off, and faltered again, recording and eventually performing. Though not photographed by Robert, accompanied by Richard, or with my brother serving attentively in the wings. I would sometimes freeze. How could Robert, Richard, Fred, and Todd, none older than forty-five, all be gone. All stripped of the possibilities of forging work, adventure and life on earth.

I was drawn back to public life through poets. Allen Ginsberg visited me in Michigan and encouraged me to take the stage with him to benefit Jewel Heart, a Tibetan Buddhist Foundation. There I met the young poet Oliver Ray, a positive source of raw Rimbaudian energy. I flew back and forth to New York where a community of friends were waiting, and we prepared the album that Fred and I had begun to map out toward the end of his life. Dedicated to Fred, our projected *Going West* would become *Gone Again.* With Lenny Kaye at the helm, we returned to Electric Lady Studios, where we had recorded *Horses.* Lenny recruited Tony Shanahan, a congenial, sensitive and invaluable musician, to play bass; he joined the core players Jay Dee Daugherty, Tom Verlaine, and Detroit pianist Luis Resto.

The title song that Fred envisioned spoken from the mouth of a tribe's matriarch transformed as a widow's song of her fallen warrior. Fred's war cries recorded at home served as a backing track. I had written *My Madrigal* reimagining the enchantment of our early courtship. Unable to complete it musically, Luis Resto, who was close to Fred, wept unashamedly as we fostered the delicate waltz together. *About a Boy,* part turbulent hymn, part improvised swirl of sound was created in the studio in remembrance of Kurt Cobain. Lenny and I wrote *Beneath the Southern Cross* over the phone, joining his circular chords with an aspirant's linear poem to life that I had written for Oliver.

The music for the centerpiece *Fireflies* was recorded live with Tom Verlaine on lead, embodying the song's restive yearning on his Jazzmaster. Jeff Buckley was at the session to prepare for a vocal and asked to be a firefly upon it. He sat on the floor with his bow, inducing the vibrations of a trembling insect on his esraj. *Fireflies* was composed by Oliver who went on to join our touring band and write some of our strongest songs. As we finished recording I expressed one last message to Fred. He had patiently taught me a handful of chords in his last months and I practiced whenever possible. I wrote him *Farewell Reel,* which I sang and played alone at album's end. We forged *Gone Again,* a work that I could hardly listen to as I had been unconscious of the aftermath of grief transported in my voice.

Walking the streets of New York I was struck with the vast amount of architectural change, whole sectors unrecognizable. I sought the familiar streets I had walked with Robert looking in the windows of pawn shops or voodoo herbalists with small bottles of sacred oils arranged among metal icons of forgotten saints. I walked aimlessly down Twenty-Second Street toward the Hudson River wearing Fred's leather bomber jacket. I felt as if I could die but knew I would just keep going. I unexpectedly collided with Annie Leibovitz. I don't know what to do, I blurted in tears. Come on, she said, my studio is just across the street, let's do some work. There was no greater remedy for me at that moment.

In September 1995 I was asked to join the International Peace Foundation in Berlin representing the arts. At the press conference I was astonished to find myself seated next to the Dalai Lama, and I recited the words to *People Have the Power.* In the next few days, I had many opportunities to be near him during greetings and conferences. Sitting across from him eating noodles as a tipsy Robert McNamara mistook him for a Japanese monk, I told him my Tibet story and the great remorse my adolescent ambition had produced. As I finished, he was called to a meeting, and I returned to my room. The light poured through the open shades as I sat thinking of my life, my dog, my prayers, my children, my widowhood. Later I would be summoned to the mezzanine. When I stepped into the elevator, His Holiness and secretary were inside, and we rode together in silence. When he arrived at his floor, his Holiness laid his hand on mine and looked intently in my eyes and said, "It was not your fault." Five words that spun all the way back to hearten a woebegone twelve-year-old girl experiencing at last the blessing of forgiveness.

When I returned to the city Allen escorted me to a dinner for William at his bunker. Allen was overjoyed that I had met His Holiness and asked me to help support the Tibetan people by performing at the annual benefit for Tibet House at Carnegie Hall. He was also determined that I return to the stage and appealed to Bob Dylan to extend his hand. Bob asked me to open him on the East Coast swing of his Paradise Lost Tour in December. Michael Stipe offered to travel with us by bus up and down the East Coast. Allen and Gregory Corso often visited us on the road. This small tour including encouraging words from Bob, boosted my confidence, brought me back to my feet.

On the third day he sent me his lyric book and asked me to choose a song to perform with him. I stayed up half the night divided between beauty and confrontation, finally choosing *Dark Eyes,* a Blakean style song of compassion and quiet dignity, the perfect one to sing side by side. Michael Stipe bought me a loosely flowing dress and braided my hair. I was somewhat nervous as Bob called me to the stage. I began the verse, and we sang the chorus together on the same microphone, our faces nearly touching. I could see tiny beads of sweat on his forehead and caught the intensity in his eyes. I gripped my dress and looked down at my bare feet, and for that moment I was just a widow and the raging young poet who once dominated my teenage senses, was just a man.

*Gone Again* was released in June 1996 with Annie's photograph of me with Fred's old jacket over my shoulder, on the cover. Clive asked we shoot a video to air on MTV. Robert Frank directed *Summer Cannibals,* Fred's song of the devouring aspects of fame, in his basement on the Bowery. The black-and-white film, unlike anything else, was not deemed MTV material and disappeared quickly. Though disappointed I felt privileged to befriend and work with a true master.

We toured around Jack and Jesse's school schedule. I had met the artist Patti Hudson at my brother's funeral. She told me that Todd had come to her in a dream as Rachael, worrying who would help me. Patti answered that call, even setting aside her own goals to assist me in my duties, eventually traveling with us shepherding Jesse. With our first major summer tour approaching I wondered how to present myself. As if in answer I received a mysterious package from Belgium, a white box tied with a black silk ribbon. Within black tissue were three white shirts, reminiscent of the shirt I had worn on the cover of *Horses,* fragile yet distinctive. Someone knows me, I thought, a stranger who makes clothes as I might have imagined. They were sent by the Flemish designer Ann Demeulemeester and became my performing shirts. She soon added a black jacket and soft black leather work boots. She had seen our concert in Brussels in 1976 when a teenager and vowed to one day make me clothes. I remembered that concert well. The response was so overwhelming I had written a poem called *The Children of Brussels.* I was touched by the revelation that Ann, soon to become a dear friend, had been one of them.

In the absence of Toddy, the band did their best as surrogate uncles. Tom Verlaine was especially good with Jack and Jesse, his childlike sense of humor transformed tedious travel into surreal playtime. I did my best to focus on the present, my goals had shifted: To provide a good living and build a collaborative body of work along the way. All the work I had done, scores of notebooks, unpublished stories, unfinished novels, were stored away. The imagined saga of the traveler who did not travel became for a time the living saga of the writer who did not write.

The spring and summer of 1997 saw the passing of both Allen Ginsberg and William Burroughs. On the afternoon of April 4th, I brought Jackson and Jesse to Allen's loft to bid farewell. He lay in his death sleep on a simple white iron bed with an old photograph of Walt Whitman above him. Those who loved him including Robert Frank, Larry Rivers, Anne Waldman, and Jonas Mekas entered the small room and stood before him to say goodbye. Gregory Corso sat for hours by his side murmuring *Oh my Allen, oh my Allen.* Monks chanted continuously. His spiritual guide Gelek Rimpoche occasionally looked in on the sleeping poet. He is holding on to life, he smiled, being a bad Buddhist. Oliver Ray and I sat by Allen's bed with his dear friend Rosebud Pettet. Peter Orlovsky spread white rose petals and prayed as Allen had instructed him. Around 2:30 a.m., Allen suddenly sat up, opened his eyes, looked at us all, then lay back down and breathed his last.

Oliver and I attended his service and then two months later flew to Lawrence, Kansas, to attend William's. The sheriff is dead, I said to no one in particular. Though his passing broke my heart, I did not shed tears. Instead, I was consumed by an excitable fury and wrote feverishly as if to bring him back, to materialize the indissoluble filament connecting us all.

*Chicago, June 1947*

# Grant

My father's favorite poem was *Abou Ben Adhem* by the British Romantic poet Leigh Hunt. He often read it aloud hardly looking at the text as if it was engrained in his heart. Conversing with an angel Abou finds himself short of inclusion in the Lord's *Book of Gold*. But cheerfully he asks if he might be included as one who loves his fellow man. This little poem seemed to speak for my father, yet he withdrew into himself, irreparably disillusioned, as mankind perpetuated unmasked cruelty.

He mourned his advancing age and that he no longer could conjure the face of May, his tragic love. I wondered if I would also experience a day when faces of people that I had cared for would fall out of focus. Stephanie or Klara or Johnny Stahl. I have no photographs of them, only vague images. I still value my life-changing teachers and schoolmates: Carol McFetridge, the best dancer. Barbara Beattie, the most creative. Billy Corsey, who introduced me to the music of Coltrane and Nina Simone. Elaine Serota, who emboldened the artist in me. Mr. Meyers, who was mocked for his stutter yet taught us of

Giuseppe Verdi and encouraged me to sing. Mr. Oberparleiter, who opened our horizons studying *Moby-Dick* and the forbidden *The Catcher in the Rye*. I think of so many others who left their mark upon me, some sadly lost to the war in Vietnam, to cancer, crime, drowning, drugs or just lost.

In the spring I would go home as much as possible to spend even a few hours with my father. At times we just sat and watched television on the couch holding hands. He wore dark shirts, black sweatpants and soft moccasins. He had few possessions, but he liked nice things. When I was young, I admired the way he held his cigarette. He let me have the empty packs: Camel straights, Turkish tobacco. They seemed exotic to me, the golden camel, palms and pyramid, the evocative foreign stamps and intriguing slogan: *I'd walk a mile for a Camel.* I loved his sonorous voice, his melancholia, his deep concentration when reading a book, reading aloud incomprehensible passages to my impatient mother trying to prepare a meal. His athletic graces, his broken pinky finger that remained bent.

I made a brief visit to see my parents before leaving for Europe. My mother was working on a jigsaw puzzle of an old mill. My father was in the backyard feeding the birds. I hesitated to disturb him but felt an urgency to see him and quietly slipped out back. He was standing at the end of the yard with his back toward me with arms outstretched. As I stood in silence the birds flew to him and covered him, as if a fresco from the painter Giotto's life cycle of St. Francis of Assisi.

I could feel the birds' affection for him, not merely because he fed them, but because they were responding to his innate goodness. At that moment I had no doubt that he was of a hallowed tribe. Not a perfect man, nor had he produced any known miracle, yet he had the simplicity of a saint, and I the saint's errant daughter. Somehow sensing my presence, he turned as the birds flew above him and looked at me.

Hello doll, he said.

Hello, Daddy, I answered.

RACING TOWARD THE MILLENNIA. The realization that the Twentieth Century, with its two terrible wars, fields of dead, its cultural revolutions, Cubism, jazz, Abstract Expressionism, rock and roll and loss upon loss coming to a close. In the summer of 1999, the band had a long concert tour ending in Tel Aviv. We were accompanied by our good friend Steven Sebring, who documented our journey with his heavy Bolex camera. On our days off in Jerusalem I rode a donkey in the hills. Steven, Oliver and I visited the Garden of Gethsemane, fenced in and smaller than I had imagined. We wended through the marketplace, one path after another, then followed the Way of Tears. I imagined the feet of Christ upon the massive stones worn smooth by the steps of centuries of pilgrims. Soldiers patrolled the Wailing Wall; in narrow alcoves men were answering the call to prayer.

Later, sitting in the debilitating desert heat in Qumran, I reread the telegram I had received from my sister. *Daddy in hospital, serious, please come home.* Our concert fell on his eighty-third birthday, but I called him at the hospital to tell him I would cancel it. He forbade me to do that, instead instructing me to read passages from the Old and New

Testaments and the Quran, appealing for unity. He promised he would wait for me.

We played in the Tel Aviv Cinerama; the atmosphere crackled with high energy, all three faiths were recognized and shown respect as my father wished. I couldn't help but feel that within the collective heart of the people there existed the same spirit of humanity he possessed, as we celebrated his birthday. That same night I had a nightmare. I was taken by the hand of an angel and was swept above the city. We stood on a high hill looking down at Jerusalem, entirely in rubble. I felt the influence of the dizzying heat. The desert will cover all, he said. It will prevail even as humankind will not.

When I returned home, my father was sitting up in his hospital bed wearing his clip-on sunglasses, my beatnik father. I told him of only the desert, the inclusive magic of the concert. My father had always searched for the meaning of life. He knew exactly when he would leave us to wander somewhere in time, as if he could calculate his days in remaining grains of sand. Accepting that he was to give up on the world was very difficult for us. Linda, ever the faithful nurse, administered his needs in her home. In the dog days of August, he said he loved us all and told my mother she had been a good wife. He died a quiet death, leaving us with the sense that we had been blessed. It was as he wished, to go discreetly and be ushered into the new world, to reclaim the vigor of youth, the hand of May and to look upon his son's face.

On my father's shelf were eleven porcelain birds. He had joined a bird of the month club; when the last one arrived my mother let me take it home. It was a simple grey turtledove, nestled in straw. It inspired the song *China Bird* on the album *Gung Ho,* a phrase meaning to work together. For the cover I chose a photograph of him when he was a soldier stationed in Townsend, Australia, before he was deployed to New Guinea. He stands confidently, one hand on his hip, ready to serve his country.

For some months I maneuvered through a thick haze of grief, a curtain that would not be pulled back. I kept moving from one place to another lighting candles, trying to speak to him across the net of the game we are all playing. I felt him in the brooding wheels turning in the waterways of Vietnam, in the forest temples in Cambodia. I saw him in the face of an icon of St. Seraphim of Sarov. I felt if I stretched my arms high enough, I could find him but could never reach that far. Then as time passed, I was confounded, as tears fell. Who was I mourning? Who was I praying to? The form of prayer that for decades was solely between me and God, divided then multiplied. Between me and Robert, then Fred, my brother, my father. Modern prayers hardly language at all. A moan, a twitch. Rebel hump where art thou? Strange sounds not entirely mine, especially in half sleep, clawing toward the new century.

*Mommy and Grampy, Upper Darby, PA*

# Peaceable Kingdom

I am the dark, the widowed, the disconsolate
I am the prince of Aquitaine whose tower is down
My only star is dead, and star configurate . . .

GÉRARD DE NERVAL

I SAT ON MY STOOP in New York and reread a poem in *The Chimeras* by Nerval that I had particularly loved when young. At the time I likened it to the image of a tarot card, the fallen tower, that drew me into its desolate atmosphere. Now it read with a relatable clarity; I am that widowed one, no one stands watch in my turret and my shoulder bears the poet's melancholy mark. I looked down the street toward an emptiness where twin towers stood only a year ago. 2001, the Kubrick year. What monolith would we now celebrate? The phone rang, my reverie was broken, I had a feeling it was my mother's daily call.

We spoke of the feel of early autumn. She was worried that the Stone Pony club in Asbury Park, where she loved to sit among adoring fans during our shows, was rumored to close. I assured her a great effort was being waged to save it. I mentioned that my voice seemed to be deepening, and I would have to drop the keys to certain songs. You'll be sounding like me soon, she laughed, like a nightclub singer. Yes, I said, it must be in my genes. She turned serious then said, Well, kid, I have a story to tell you about genetics when I see you. I urged her to tell me on the phone, but she refused. Oh no, she said, I'll tell you in person this weekend.

I was consumed with curiosity but would have to wait. A few days later, my mother fell, hit her head and lost consciousness. I boarded the next bus to South Jersey and joined Linda at the hospital. A blood clot had been found; the operation successful, but for a while she remained distant and confused. After her recovery when I tried to approach the subject of genetics, she stared at me blankly. She had no idea what I was talking about. I wondered if it might relate to a rumor concerning my paternity, that circulated among my mother's side of the family. It had been fueled by my great-grandmother and waved away by both my parents. I had hoped she might bring the subject up again, but my mother was never quite the same after her fall. Her world was tethered to her faith and an increased longing to return to the realm of childhood, to reunite with her mother and father.

She underwent physical therapy then was transferred to the local hospital shortly before the first anniversary of September 11th. They replayed the fall of the towers over and over on the small television. I thought of the horror I felt on September 11th. I had sent Jesse off to school and lay down for a bit and dozed off. The phone rang and a dear friend called in alarm, shouting get dressed, go in the basement, we've been attacked. I rose quickly and panicked, thinking of Jesse only a few blocks away and sped to the school. As I hit the street I saw the smoke. I watched horrified as one of the towers collapsed. The air was already filled with white dust, ashes, part architecture, part human. Consumed with the safety of my daughter was the most frightening moment of my life.

Between giving birth to four children and operations my mother was no stranger to hospitals. She never seemed to mind; in fact, she liked being taken care of, a respite from endless responsibilities. After six days she looked at us and said she didn't think she was going to make it this time. On the evening of the 17th, we all had hoagies, a South Jersey staple, and for a brief time we seemed a happy family. All we need is Toddy, I said. The television was on—my mother had always slept with it on, waiting for my father to return from the night shift. I glanced at it just as a movie was starting; it was an English science fiction rarely broadcast, *The Day of the Triffids*. It was one of Toddy's favorite movies. It's Toddy! we all agreed; he is here. Linda's family, all Jehovah's Witnesses, magnified my mother's faith. I was grateful she had Linda by her side, whispering gently. My mother truly believed and left us with her vision of paradise.

As was her wish, my mother was buried next to Todd, her beloved son. The loss of my mother hit me much harder than I had imagined. I sat weeping, holding one of the last books she sent to me. *Sara Crewe.* She was, in a sense, my fairy godmother, like the blue fairy that watched over Pinocchio, even as he trespassed again and again. The death of our parents rearranges our universe, for a while things swing out of balance, and one experiences a dizzying orphaned sensation. My mother's passing filled me with the sense of something left unsaid. Yet she had inscribed my copy of *Sara Crewe* with the phrase *We need no words.* But had we words enough? Had I really loved her enough? Did I give her all the time she deserved? I have often wished for one more hour, to sit with her at the kitchen table drinking coffee fully attending to her fanciful often-told stories.

THE TWENTY-FIRST CENTURY had not unfolded as my generation had once envisioned: universal harmony, renunciation of war, charity according to the need. In the wake of the devastating assault of the Twin Towers, one could sense an insidious rise in nationalism, a desire for retaliation and revenge. My private hopes for peace and openness in Israel and Palestine were also deteriorating. I dreaded the possibility of future catastrophic destruction prophesized in the nightmare I had when I was in Jerusalem, that I had withheld from my father.

On October 26, 2002, International A.N.S.W.E.R. organized a protest of the planned attack on Iraq by the Bush administration in Washington, D.C. I attended with Oliver Ray to join several speakers including the Reverend Jesse Jackson, Jessica Lange, Susan Sarandon and Reverend Al Sharpton. Steven Sebring accompanied us to shoot footage. After a plea for no war, Oliver and I performed *People Have the Power*. An estimated 200,000 gathered from all over the country; looking back from the Constitution Gardens near the Vietnam War Memorial, the mall was carpeted with people calling for peace, chanting no war. We met again in January, performing in the freezing cold, joining forces with Reverend Jesse Jackson. On February 15th the largest global anti-war protest in history was waged. In England alone nearly a million protested, in Italy a staggering three million. Sadly, the collective voice of the people was not heeded.

On March 16, 2003, Rachael Corrie, a young nonviolence activist was protesting the Israeli demolition of homes in the Gaza Strip. Bulldozers had already destroyed surrounding houses in Rafah where she was based; they targeted the family home of Professor Nasrallah where she was staying. Corrie, wearing an orange vest, bullhorn in hand, called for them to cease. She stood on a raised mound in the path of an Israeli bulldozer, but it kept going. Her fellow activists cried out and the Nasrallah children watched in horror as she was crushed to death. The loss of Corrie, a bright altruistic force, just two years older than my own son, haunted me. At the same time, it was obvious that all the marches, pleas and protests of millions of people worldwide were not going to halt the Bush administration's plan to attack Baghdad.

On March 19th, the anniversary of my mother's birthday, I lay with the worst migraine of my life. From the floor below I could hear the news. We were preparing to bomb Baghdad, Operation Shock and Awe. Jon Lee Anderson, an embedded journalist for *The New Yorker,* reported that before the bombing, the birds fell silent, failing to herald the first day of spring.

There was nothing of my experience in life as physically painful and all-consuming as that migraine. I thought of my mother suffering such migraines and my resentment as a child having to tend to her. I attempted to displace my thoughts, disassociate from the pain. I was thinking of Virginia Woolf, who suffered cluster migraines, pulling her into a spiral of hallucination, a relentless chorus of voices and unspeakable misery. To distract myself, I spent hours in the dark composing a long poem in my head. Leaping from the silence of birds to Virginia and her sister Vanessa to Linda and me. I entered the realm of a mother singing her children to sleep, comforting them as the bombs fell in her city. I lay, in the throes of migraine, thinking of the women of Baghdad, the cradle of civilization, cradling their children.

All day and through the night I remained in my shuttered room. After eighteen hours the migraine slowly subsided, resulting in my poem, *Birds of Iraq*. Our efforts to halt the bombing had been ineffectual, my only recourse was to respond through work. Susan Sontag, a longtime friend of mine and Robert's, had kindly written the liner notes for my last Arista release, a compilation, *Land (1975–2002)*. When I spoke to her of my idea for recording a response to the Bush administration's invasion of Iraq, Susan impressed upon me the importance of studying history to understand how modern conflicts are fueled. As she had advised, I studied the history and contributions of Iraq in preparation for the improvisational composition *Radio Baghdad*. I adopted a mother's view, one that could not be politically dissected. Susan had just been diagnosed with blood cancer and was waging her own battle and I thought of her as we recorded live, opening with the sounds of Iraqi children playing and driven by Oliver Ray's explosive chord structure as sorrow spiraled as reproach.

In the spring of 2004, *Trampin',* my first album on Columbia, was released. Lenny Kaye and I composed the opening song *Jubilee,* calling the people to face troubled times together. Lenny, Jay Dee, Tony Shanahan, and Oliver Ray all contributed to create our song *Gandhi,* conveying his message for peace and independence. Tony Shanahan wrote the music for the songs *Mother Rose* in memory of my mother and *Peaceable Kingdom* for Rachael Corrie. We recorded the title track, a spiritual sung by Marian Anderson, live at The Looking Glass Studios. My daughter Jesse played the piano with unadorned grace, her debut in a studio and our first time recording together. I chose *Trampin'* as the title for the album as it appeals to the simplicity of spiritual faith and the path of the weary vagabond.

At year's end Susan Sontag's valiant fight with leukemia had come to an end. Now her body of work would speak for her. I flew to Paris for her funeral and stayed in the apartment that she had shared with Annie Leibovitz in the room that had been Susan's study. Unable to sleep, I read her copy of Baudelaire's *Intimate Journals.* I thought of Susan through the years dancing during my concerts, scolding me for having a messy library and counseling me to read more German writers which led me to Hermann Broch and Thomas Bernhard. I thought of Susan's lust for beauty, her suffering, her elastic mind, and desire for heightened experiences.

In early morning on the day of the funeral a cold mist rose from the Seine and surrounded Notre-Dame. I walked up the street and stopped at 7 rue des Grands Augustins, the studio where Picasso painted *Guernica*. Susan had told me that it was the same studio that Balzac had chosen to place his character the painter Frenhofer in *The Unknown Masterpiece*.

All convened at the Montparnasse Cemetery, passing the bronze statue of the Angel of Eternal Sleep that rises above its center. At gravesite a car pulled up, and a small woman emerged. I noted the thrust of her arm, a thick shock of short wavy hair, and a heart-shaped determined face. It was the French actress Nicole Stéphane. I had seen photographs of her with Jean Cocteau and had loved her as Elisabeth in Jean-Pierre Melville's *Les Enfants Terribles*. Fearless, singular Nicole. She joined Annie and close friend and caretaker, Sharon Delano. I stood back observing them, three strong and accomplished women, devoted to Susan, all giving something of themselves on her behalf. It was quite cold, and snow was forming. Annie asked me to return the following day and take a picture of the grave. It was laden with flowers including a wreath from the mayor of Susan's chosen city of Paris. It had stopped snowing; I took a picture with my Polaroid camera and gave the image to Annie as she bid.

A few months later I joined my friends Alain Lahana, Andy Woolliscroft and Ann Demeulemeester on Proust's birthday in the outskirts of Paris for the Solidays Festival. There on the festival grounds Minister of Culture Renaud Donnedieu de Vabres presented me the medal Commandeur des Arts et des Lettres. In my twenties I had admired William

Burroughs's Commandeur fleurette that he proudly wore on his lapel. You will also have one someday, he said with certainty. When the medal, on a wide green and white ribbon, was placed around my neck, I thought of his unexpected prophesy as well as Susan who had received the same honor. But mostly I thought of that eight-year-old girl who vowed one day to get her own medals.

Afterwards I visited Nicole Stéphane in her Paris apartment. I brought my guitar and sang to her. She gave me two gifts. Her mother's copy of Milton's *Poetical Works* in English and a small pillow with a sketch of her by Jean Cocteau. But the greatest gift was her trust and acceptance. She was not well but spent time with me and told me of her life. She was born a baroness in the Rothschild family, in the realm of wealth, a blond, black sheep entwined in the arts. In World War II she joined the French Resistance and was imprisoned. She spoke of her affair with Susan, her sorrows. As I was leaving, she told me a friend of hers had recently died. They said Kaddish for him, she said, but I am alone, who will say Kaddish for me? I wasn't certain what Kaddish was, but I silently vowed that I would honor her in some way when the time came.

The first decade of the new century proved to be a frenetic one of work, travel, death and accolades. When I first reentered public life, I had limited my concert touring around Jackson and Jesse's school schedule. Now that they were grown, my touring and travel increased. A memorable event was the opportunity to curate the annual London Meltdown Festival. In calling it Innocence and Experience, we paid homage to our cultural heritage from William Blake to Jimi Hendrix. A prime intent was in creating solidarity by bringing together veteran and fledgling. We invited musicians, poets, and war correspondents for two weeks of diverse and heightened performances. For my personal contribution I hoped to work with Kevin Shields, the visionary founder of My Bloody Valentine. I asked him if he would consider improvising a live track to my reading of *The Coral Sea,* a suite of poems I had written for Robert shortly after he died. We spoke together for several hours, a celestial conversation, with no rehearsal. Our performance was based on mutual trust. I had never performed the piece, and was soon overwhelmed with emotion, recalling writing it at the kitchen table, in a state of suspended grief. Enveloped by the cathedral-like layers of Kevin's sonic looping I surrendered and dropped the text on the floor. I no longer needed it, as I knew how to express within the language of poetry Robert's transfiguration. That performance exceeded my hopes of merging poetry with pure sound, a language of its own. The last evening John Cale performed, followed by our premiere of *Horses* in its entirety. I thought it fitting as *Horses* was bred in an innocent time and we did our best to now deliver it infused with experience.

The band toured Europe, South America, Australia, Japan, Istanbul, Morocco, Seoul. Everywhere I went I took my manuscript that would become *Just Kids*. Consulting a vivid memory and countless diaries and journals, I wrote, rewrote and often struggled with the immense responsibility to Robert and the city where our story unfolded. When we were twenty, we created a running game that we called *our story*. At night I would often read to him or tell a childhood story. One night when snow was falling, he said sleepily, tell me our story. It began with a girl with a plaid suitcase, searching for a place to stay and finding a sleeping boy, who sensing her presence, opened his eyes and smiled. Each time he asked I would add our new adventures until he'd fall asleep. When he asked me to write *our story,* hours before he died, I knew exactly what he wanted me to do.

In my sixtieth year, I was inducted into the Rock & Roll Hall of Fame where I venerated my bandmates, my brother, Fred, and especially my mother due to her devotion to our music and the people. Steven Sebring completed the film he had laboriously pieced together, a decade of my life. The children grew in the radiant blur of our travels. London. Tokyo. Jerusalem. The graves of William Blake, Keats, Shelley, and Arthur Rimbaud. Anti-war protests in Washington, D.C. Singing the blues with Sam Shepard. Laughing with Flea on the beach, and the vanishing landscape of Michigan. Ten years of filming our sprawling patchwork. *Dream of Life* was presented at the Berlin Film Festival, aired on PBS, and was nominated for an Emmy. The Cartier Foundation in Paris presented Land 250, my first major solo exhibition representing five fields: photography, drawing, installations, performance, and poetry. Within it was an installation in memory of Robert incorporating the track of *The Coral Sea*. Yet I still had not yet completed our story as I promised. I continued my journeys with the manuscript in my small metal suitcase. Robert and I never traveled in life, but now we went everywhere together.

In 2009 after a heavy touring schedule I stayed on in Paris. In the Jewish sector of Père-Lachaise, I located the sepulture of Baron Henri de Rothschild, where Nicole was buried. As she desired, I recited Kaddish, the Jewish prayer for the dead, for her. I also returned to the Montparnasse Cemetery and visited Susan, noticing clouds reflecting in the gleaming black surface of her headstone. Turning a corner, I found the resting place of Samuel Beckett. There was a single rose lying on his marker.

–Thank you for your work, thank you for Godot. We're all waiting for the universe to answer us.

–Oh! an answer will come, a voice replied, but the wait is long.

–I don't mind, I said.

I was desperate to finish my book and decided to stay in Europe, where I was given the time and solitude I needed. I stayed in a converted chapel in the South of France, part of a compound that belonged to dear friends. The chapel was small, monastic with stained-glass windows, a bed and a desk. When I grew restless, I explored the grounds of their complex

and discovered ancient olive trees and a gypsy wagon. Within
the wagon was a small table, with votive candles and an image
of Arthur Rimbaud. I labored over the final edits of the book I
had promised Robert, chiseling last bits of marble. The chapel
was at last strewn with the glittering dust of completion. I was
soon to leave; I had been up until dawn writing what had to be
written, thankful it looked to be a glad day. An arc of rose-
colored light spread across the stone floor. My rebel hump had
not abandoned me but had seemingly flowed through my pen
scratching across the last pages.

We wage the fever of disappointment, the realization that
yesterday's crumbling tower was not a fantasy, that like the
Prince of Aquitaine one is hurled and drawn like a human
tarot card. How can we leap back up? Get back on our feet,
grab a cart, and start gathering the debris, both physical and
emotional. Crush it into small stones, then pulverize them and
as the dust settles, dance upon it. How do we do that? By
returning to our child self, weathering our obstacles in good
faith. For children operate in the perpetual present, they go on,
rebuild their castles, lay down their casts and crutches, and
walk again.

*Midway Musical Bar, Philadelphia, 1943*

# A Drop of Blood

IT WAS TEN YEARS since our mother's passing. I took a train to Philadelphia and Linda was waiting for me at the station. She had made Artisan loaves and we sat in her kitchen having warm bread and coffee. The question of my lineage had been stored away but was rekindled that afternoon. Going through some of our mother's belongings, Linda discovered a small box of unseen photographs, mostly pictures from her childhood, and one of herself at twenty with a teenage boy. On the back was written *Bev and cousin Joey,* the youngest child of her Uncle Joe. Linda showed me the photograph, we could easily have been mistaken for brother and sister. The likeness was uncanny. I bore no resemblance to my father or his side of the family and was excited to find someone I clearly looked like.

We became aware some years ago that my great-grandmother suspected I was the child of her oldest son, Joe. The rumor floated within my mother's side of the family but wasn't taken seriously. We reasoned that if it was true Joey would be indeed my half-brother. To settle all speculation

Linda and I decided to take a genetic test. She pricked my finger, and then her own, using the same method we had as children with our brother in the woods by a stream surrounded by jack-in-the-pulpits, skunk cabbages and dragonflies. Huddled together we pressed our tiny wounds against one another's, pledging our youthful vows of loyalty, eternally to keep. My sister put our two drops of blood into a prepared envelope and sent it out for evaluation. We hoped this singular action would either quell or confirm my great-grandmother's suspicions about my paternity.

The results arrived several weeks later. Linda took a train to New York. She was holding the sealed manila envelope. Within minutes we were standing on the street corner, examining two sets of incomprehensible numbers. It seemed that our blood, compared and interpreted by science, disclosed that we were most likely half siblings. As if pulled apart, we wept. Holding both hands, we assured one another that it didn't matter.

As for my great-grandmother, I could forgive how she treated me, but not my poor mother, who she denied even the smallest measure of affection. If her accusations were true, I was a full member of the Williams tribe, a mix of Celtic and Welsh. I held to my sole memory of meeting my great-uncle Joe at a family reunion. I was about four and found myself drawn to him and climbed the porch steps and uncharacteristically sat on his lap. I remember Grammie shouting to my mother to retrieve me. She hurried up the porch shading her eyes as she spoke to him. I'm sorry, Joe, she said, and took my hand. I waved to him, and he winked and smiled. I never saw him again but if he proved to be my father, it was a memory to cherish.

The results of our test put a great strain on my thought processes and for some time I was unable to write. Every morning without fail I had sat in a local café with my notebook and coffee, now I was obliged to question the validity of what I had written. Ironically, I had thought to entitle my manuscript *Truth,* as I fancied the idea of a one-word title that defined my purpose. Only now a shadow of half-truth loomed over the entire work. A phrase of Jean Genet's from *What Remains of a Rembrandt* rolled back and forth, a crushing insistent wave. *What I have just written is false.* As a reader I was shocked and confused by his words, as a writer I recoiled at the sentiment that those words may also be mine.

The pen ceases to scratch. My rebel hump is helmet shaped, as if from a suit of armor. It is my hood of fleece, preserving solitude, a sense of anonymity. A breastplate protecting my heart. It is pre-knowledge. A withered cloak, or a leaf passed from generation to generation. It is surrendering to a scientific method, a drop of blood.

Some months before my seventieth birthday, attempting to track the genetic origins of our mother's side, Linda and I took an autosomal DNA test. It was a simpler test, tracing ancestral origins, merely requiring a vial of saliva. Until then, we had kept our findings to ourselves and considered the case closed. I had all but accepted the fact that I was fathered by my mother's Uncle Joe, and fully expected the results to confirm it.

My sister's test arrived first, as anticipated it verified her genealogy: Celtic from the Williams side and Scotch-Irish from the Smiths. I expected that my lineage would be predominantly Celtic and tried to be enthusiastic, though I still secretly hoped the outcome might show an error in our previous blood test. The results of my test were delayed, arriving on the morning of my seventieth birthday. Once again, I would be obliged to rearrange my entire universe.

One prick of a finger and the lid had flipped open, a sheet of paper with endless numerical combinations revealing Linda and I as half siblings. But it was a vial of saliva that exposed the undisputable truth of my paternal source. All fanciful scenarios of my origins evaporated in seconds. I was not from Neverland, nor a tribe from the remotest section of the American desert. I was not planted in a womb by an alien race, nor left in a basket beneath the western sky. Nor was I born of the woolgatherers or a nineteenth-century poet. It was not even my mother's kindly Uncle Joe who once set me on his lap. My paternal ancestors were driven from Russia to the Ukraine, from Kiev to Shpola, then embarked from Liverpool to Newfoundland, finally taking root in Philadelphia. I was most likely conceived in Philadelphia not long after the close of World War II. We had inadvertently unraveled my mother's furtive past. My blood father was from a line of wanderers, uprooted and replanted to spring elsewhere, one hundred percent Ashkenazi.

In a time of a self-imposed sabbatical, I researched side by side with the most trustworthy and altruistic assistant. In the passing years, I had been blessed to reunite with the child that I had placed in adoption when I was twenty. A resolutely private person, she was embraced and welcomed into our fold. A great amount of sleuthing had brought her back to us, and it was she who pinpointed the identity of my blood father, her grandfather. After several months of exhaustive research, we had a name, a regiment, a birthplace, but not his photograph.

On Independence Day I did not feel well. There were sounds of distant fireworks; I was unable to sleep. I sat for hours going backward within myself, cell by cell in search of him, in search of what aspects of myself were him. Without real design or foresight, I took a deep dive into the brain of my computer. Propped up by several pillows I cross-referenced every clue we had gathered about my blood father. As the night dragged on the city beyond became strangely silent, emptied of revelers. I grew tired but the desire to see his face kept me going. And then around 4 a.m., just as I was about to give up, I chanced upon a PDF of a file copy of *The Torretta Flyer* from Redondo Beach, California. In the section called The Last Mission were three deceased soldiers. I knew he was my father when I saw his face, a young gunner, with dark wavy hair, hands in pockets before white-washed barracks in Bari, Italy. His name was Sidney. I saw my young self in his stance, his insolent gaze, and stared at his image until dawn, unknown yet present as the new moon caught in the corridors between the edges of the earth and sun.

ON MARCH 19, 1946, Beverly Ann Williams sat at a bar smoking a cigarette, perhaps listening to *The Gypsy* by the Ink Spots, the most popular song at the time. Throughout the war, she worked as a waitress, hatcheck girl, cigarette girl, and sometimes sang in nightclubs. It was her birthday; she was twenty-six years old. She lost her mother at eleven and experienced very little love without her. She had been obliged to grow up fast, raised by a grandmother who had four sons of her own and no use for a granddaughter.

By twenty-three, she had survived one annulled marriage and one abusive marriage. She lost a son in a botched delivery and nearly died of childbed fever. After she recovered, she folded all the baby clothes and placed them in a box to donate to the poor. With nowhere to go, she appealed to her Uncle Joe, widowed and living with his teenage son; he offered her room and board in exchange for keeping house. My mother was grateful, though Grammie considered it disgraceful that she was living with a widower twice her age.

As World War II ended, two soldiers returned to Philadelphia. A handsome gunner from the 766th Bombardment Squadron and my father, Grant Harrison Smith, arriving from the jungles of the Philippines, recovering from malaria. In the center was a pretty, energetic and loving young woman. Perhaps she had known the gunner from one of the nightclubs where she worked. At the same time, she rekindled a youthful friendship with the fellow she had had a crush on as a teenager. Grant had been in love with his cousin May, who ended their long clandestine affair by sending him a Dear John letter shortly before war's end. He returned cast off by May and discovering his beloved mother was suffering with terminal cancer. Distraught he found comfort in my mother. She was compassionate, made him laugh, brought him back to life; she was his rescuer. She was good at that.

Only my mother knows the truth of those few weeks when I was conceived in early spring of 1946. Grant had left to care for his dying mother. Alone on her birthday, it's very likely she met the young gunner in a nightclub. Because of a providential chain of events: the absence of Grant, the death of Jessie Pollard Smith on Palm Sunday, the youthful restlessness of my mother in a chance postwar reunion, I was brought into the world as myself.

When my mother discovered she was pregnant, there was no doubt between her and my father that it was his. Unbeknownst to all, Grammie had searched Joe's house while my mother was working, and found an undergarment in Uncle Joe's bed, erroneously validating her suspicion that my mother was carrying on with her eldest son. My great-grandmother was so sure that the baby was fathered by Joe that she took it upon herself to confront him, which he laughingly denied. She then visited my father, accusing my mother of entrapping him. Unwittingly her meddling strengthened my father's steadfast defense of my mother.

The situation became so dire that they left Philadelphia and took a train to Chicago in the first days of summer. Getting Grant to stand by her was easy but convincing him to tie the knot was not. After five years of war, lingering malaria, and the death of his mother, he was not quite ready to take on such responsibility. As she told it, they sat on the courthouse steps for some time until he finally mustered the courage to ask for her hand, perhaps for the sake of their child, and they wed in a simple civil ceremony.

As they boarded the train to Chicago, all characters

involved in my pre-birth drama receded in the distance. Grant and Beverly Smith found a rooming house near Logan Square which was somewhat squalid at the time. There I began my life, that was thankfully saved, through the efforts of my father, who held me for hours above a steaming washtub, so I could breathe.

All these facts were well-known family lore. But nowhere within them was the story of a handsome Jewish pilot. I can only wonder if the story my mother promised to tell me about genetics may have been about him. All our bits of information, like crumbs on a wayward path, were gathered by my eldest and me, magnified by my newfound first cousin, a prominent architect and scholar named Anthony Alofsin. His beautiful mother, Eleanor, Sidney's sister, had been a concert pianist. Anthony was fond of my father and I was able to fit his recollections into the puzzle of my parentage. Finding Anthony who was born only a week after my brother Todd was truly like finding another half sibling. Our parents had grown up together and we both were deeply moved to have each other in our lives.

Sidney had lost his father at the age of six during the Spanish flu pandemic. He loved to travel, appreciated art and jazz. He studied electrical engineering but was coerced into the family's successful hide and tanning business by his domineering mother. He was also forbidden, with the threat of disinheritance, to date outside of their faith. Because of this, he could never have developed any kind of meaningful relationship with my mother.

Somewhere along the line he met a Catholic, French-Canadian girl named Marie, a sweet, devoted companion he was unable to marry. In January 1965, after his mother's funeral, Sidney and sweetheart Marie wed, and they were at last blessed with mutual happiness. Though childless, they had one another. They celebrated his fifty-third birthday by the sea, but fate was not kind to them. Sidney had suffered kidney damage during the war and died tragically that November, never reaching their first anniversary. Marie, only eleven months a bride, now a widow, lived to be ninety. Had I known of her years ago, I would have certainly requested a visit with her, brought her flowers and listened intently to her recollections of her husband, my father. I think of her living out her life without his presence, but surely, she felt him in the air she breathed. Having been widowed at forty-seven, I have felt a stoic kinship with her, and place her on my wall of heroines, those who shouldered cruel providence and kept going. I was able to locate her modest headstone, simply engraved with her married name.

My sister and I had to reconcile the fact that we were only half-sisters. For a time, it made us unconsolably sad, but Linda, ever wise, told me that she had a sudden epiphany. She reminded me that the person she loved, being me, was only that person because she was conceived by my mother and Sidney, that I would not exist had it not been for him. Perhaps from him I had received the traits she adored in me: his dark hair, his swagger, his appetite for travel, culture, art, Paris and the sea. We came to care for Sidney together. I cherish the few precious photos of him in uniform, standing before the Eiffel

Tower, and another with Marie. In time, not only could I feel him, but I also felt certain that my father loved me just the same. I admired my mother's silence; she knew I favored my father, and instead of resenting this, she shielded me from the fact that he had not fathered me. And so, we came to express gratitude for my mother's postwar misadventure.

There are no hands extended, no hands turning on memory's most prevalent clock. I see a train of humanity stumble through vast plains, the people of my father, moving from place to place. I feel for them as I feel for those driven from Tibet, Syria, Palestine. And perhaps that is the true value of my ancestral blood, feeling empathy for the exiled. The keel of an overturned vessel barely detectable in a passive, if not dead sea. I wish nothing more than to freeze it with an old Leica and tape the image of its blurred silhouette to the wall of an empty room overlooking the ruins of a late nineteenth-century apartment building. Europe after the war, with dazed and famished homeless stopping to look up as though feeling my presence.

My room would be devoid of anything, save a card table with one chair, with stray shafts of wheat and hay laid out in a corner, ample enough for sleeping. I would have a blanket of taupe colored felt, the same material that Joseph Beuys draped himself with as he slept aside a coyote, in a corner of a room not far removed from my imagined refuge. I would sit at the table and write in my journal. Pencils, a pitcher of water, a small glass, and a sandwich wrapped in wax paper. At nightfall I would drink cold coffee; pace then lie wrapped in my blanket on my mat.

I would trace the women who I would never meet, Marie or Jessie or my own grandmother Marguerite, small, playful, green-eyed, musical, and light of step. The only child of a prominent New England family, she ran off with a young soldier, as handsome as she was pretty. Her father disowned her, and she was never to see her parents again. How terrible for this sunny little thing, fun-loving and kind, who loved silent films and pretty dresses. One morning, no longer able to recognize her daughter, Marguerite lunged at her wielding a kitchen knife. She was taken to a hospital then transferred to an asylum. There she was abandoned by her family and left in the old Norristown State Hospital trapped like Artaud or Frances Farmer, in the psychiatric ward. In keeping with the times, she was subjected to new shock experiments and insulin treatments; schizophrenic patients were all treated by putting them in insulin-induced comas. She never was to return, dying in the asylum at the age of forty-four. I open the case of the century-old mandolin of Marguerite. Along with *Silver Pennies* these were the sole belongings in my mother's possession, animating a brief life devoted to poetry and music. Perhaps I have just a breath of my grandmother's madness, protected yet enhanced by the capability to transform such breath into art.

Everything that happens years before we are born sets the stage for our existence. How happy I am that the throw of dice, from so far afield, begat the circumstance for me to be born. Rearranging pieces, tiny bits of truths revealed. Standing in a patch of dried vegetation, cacti, desert flowers under a sky vomiting stars, I chant the same words as my ancestors, feeling a sense of human continuity.

One quiet afternoon I was sitting at my desk, my mind wandering. It was in that moment I saw him. He wore a dark suit and a tie. I was wearing my blue Easter coat with a lace collar. Uncle Bobby had taken me to the Philadelphia Zoo. He sat me on a bench by Bird Lake and promised to return very soon. Then someone took my hand, and we went for a walk. I noticed that everyone smiled as we passed, and I felt proud to walk with him. We went for a ride in a boat shaped like a swan; I felt a wave of happiness. When the boat docked my uncle was waiting and he helped me disembark, only I mis-stepped and my shoes filled with water. I turned and looked back and saw a face that was mine: dark brows, dark hair and a gaze fixed elsewhere. I am your gait, I breathed, your smile, your off-center eye. The last piece, the blood of my mosaic.

*Air force base, Bari, Italy*

"Patti" — March 8, 1947

# Snapshots

When morning comes and "Patti" wakes,
She opens up her eyes —
She looks upon each new day —
With such complete surprise.

### II

First she'll yawn and stretch her arms
away above her head
Then she'll smile as she watches the sun
Play hide and seek across her bed.

### III

She's like a tiny rose bud, that's been
Kissed, by the morning dew —
When she opens up her sleepy eyes
To greet each day anew.

### IV

When evening shadows came and the
Sun descends behind the purple mist
Patti closes her sleepy eyes again
To await the sun's morning kiss.

### V

Then all over again it starts
At the beginning of dawns new day
As her hands reach for the morning sun,
Happy and eager to play.

Mother

# Vagabondia

FOR A LONG TIME I maintained a vestige of innocence, a feathery wisp adrift somewhere inside me, affording me a generous measure of enthusiasm, tempering loss and disappointment. I held a constancy with my youthful calling, a blood vine circling the ankle of a twelve-year-old girl, a messenger attaching his wing and bruising her heel. I felt blessed with the aspiration to produce worthy work. But recently I've sensed a pulling away, mercurial droplets tapping my skull as I fitfully seek sleep. My ears press against the pillow, a repeating phrase pulsating: *We who no longer believe.* When did I write that, and why? It disturbs me. Have I really felt that for more than a few sullen moments?

Strung-out characters of the alphabet do their perverse dance. Bach in the background, precise notes flowing, a horizon of mathematics. My coffee grows cold, as the lively café slowly empties. I become acutely aware of my hand resting on the edge of a blank page. Fate and experience traceable in the mystical anatomy of my open palm, heavily lined and young simultaneously. I grip a drying pen and seek to unearth a kernel of truth, accomplishing very little. Subjective truth cannot change the course of things nor dispel the fury of nature. It is the direct result of horror morphing into shame. I order another coffee, more people, less people, making little impact on my productivity; somehow the day disappears.

Later that night, preparing for sleep, I feel a warmth spreading across my face. At first it frightens me, as if overcome with fever, but then I empty myself in a rare moment of surrender. A dialogue seems to fill the room, unbidden, enlightening.

–What is God?

–Presence in the face of suffering.

My sister comes to mind. Those who believe.


There is a full moon and a partial lunar eclipse. A dark and murky bruise slowly invades a portion of the bright sphere. Everything stops for a moment, as if existing within a page of a graphic novel. Stop-action begetting pages of stop-action. KAPOW!! Know Thyself! Believe! The indisputable proof lies in the invisible, marking hearts with hardcore hope.

Saint Bernadette sacrificed all expectations of companionship, of children. She clawed the earth, baring a healing spring, whose waters were denied to her. Dying young, her sole reward in life was the visitations of the Virgin and the promise of happiness in the afterlife. Joan of Arc was led to the stake; her Saints did not intervene as the flames engulfed her, nor did Jesus as she called out his name. She was afforded a greater gift than earthly salvation—the truth of her Voices. John the

Revelator, the unfathomable patron of all revelations, labored to transcribe prophesy in a cave in Patmos. Fortified by the source of his vision, he was struck with a divinely instructed announcement, streaming from seven directions, connecting like tiny glowing bulbs of an interminable pinball machine.

Consider the labor of the material visionary. A mathematician's sudden moment of insight, an incontestable equation that nonetheless must be proved, setting in motion the grueling process of formulating the abstract. The artist stabilizes an aspect of the flow of metamorphosis, to freeze as a work of art. Da Vinci's *Last Supper,* Piero della Francesca's *The Legend of the True Cross,* or *Blue Poles* by Jackson Pollock. We enter the psyche of the process by observing then surrendering to the artist's articulated vision.

I search my shelves for a particular catalogue, a souvenir from a recent visit to the Sansevero Chapel in Naples. There are several images of Giuseppe Sanmartino's masterpiece, *The Veiled Christ,* taken from different angles. The marble Christ lies in his death sleep, a shroud covering his face and body, disturbingly transparent, exposing his suffering. At his feet are shackles, nails and pliers, perfectly wrought instruments of his torment. Studying these moving images, I am easily transported back to Naples, reliving the extraordinary hour that I spent within the chapel. As I stood over the imitation of the Messiah, I detected an innate disquiet in the glowing patina of his features and though forbidden I ran my fingers over his wound and a portion of the shroud. I felt the vibrations of an inaudible yet exquisite moan and was carried through time to the genesis of the sculptor's creation. I shadowed him as he searched for the perfect model. Believing to have found him, he trails him, noting his habits, body language, and the play of light on his neck and the muscles of his limbs. He is excessively mobile, no sooner reaching his destination, then preparing to leave. Nevertheless, the sculptor chooses him to embody the dead Christ. He offers him work but explains he must lie perfectly still, for hours on end, completely against his nature. In return he will be paid one gold ducat, and the promise of immortality.

Obliged to emulate death, the restless and agitated model explores his untapped psyche, then emboldened, cell by cell he permeates the consciousness of Christ. I observed all of this and wrote quickly, detailing the unholy metamorphoses, stopping short as the model melded with the coiling fibers of the Messiah's mind. I became acutely aware of astonished onlookers around me and was obliged to close my notebook and reenter the present. All were commenting on the miracle of the shroud; one could well imagine the reactions in the mid-eighteenth century. The people, mystified by its perfection, universally believed Raimondo di Sangro, the famed alchemist who commissioned the work, had melded a gauzelike material and alchemically marbleized it over the face and body of the Christ. This speculation was regarded as fact for well over two centuries. There should have been no question that it was the work of a divinely inspired and technically brilliant sculptor. A great artist is an alchemist as well, driven to transfigure the beauty and brutality of existence.

The golden chain of solidarity reaches throughout time. The braided clouds are stacked in the sky. This field of divine

consciousness is a fluid field, tapped and spoken of here. The alchemy of being is as complex as a flower with a golden head filled with seeds, as fingers pressed into the belly of a thief, of a host of renegade children slashing their shins with small ceremonial knives. I wonder now if I had kept going, removing myself completely, might I have entered the mind of the young man as he entered the mind of Christ. I have since tried to break that barrier, but to no avail. I went as far as I could. Perhaps I had only half lived the moment at hand, gazing inward, casting a blind eye without, with a racing universe within. In a flash I was gifted an entire history: a young man, the sculptor and the alchemist, in a one-act play extending into forever.

This process, at times paralyzing, isolates one within an impenetrable bubble. Only a child tugging at my sleeve could fully rouse me and break the spell that can extend from moments to hours. These stretches, when I seem to have gone elsewhere, harken back to that schoolgirl amazed, confused, looking down at her shoes. A frustrated teacher, an exasperated mother, a worried sibling. Where were you, they ask. Nowhere, I answer, just a vast territory dotted with spectacular boulders, animated statues, deserts, decidedly American, marshes, snow falling upon the sea. I had my own vessel with half sails, like the *Santiago,* the smallest and most agile of Magellan's fleet. I took my siblings with me and there was no hesitation on their part, no questions asked, not a shred of disbelief, our fuel through our whole lives. Occasionally there is music, a dissonant melody a song mapping the notes of the secret language of a child. Where was I? In the realm of innocence, communing with the king of tortoises, my telepathic toothbrush, the whispering weed trees.

2

The high crosses of last century's telegraph lines sweep through miles of flatlands. Are they aware of their spiritual dignity and their effect on a traveler? I summon a story of their origin, the tree sacrificed, the logger who felled it, the thoughts of the young worker atop the pole, stringing miles of cable across a barren landscape. That is something I can do, sit quietly, go elsewhere and not return empty-handed. I long for that, but presently a step further, go elsewhere physically, sit by the window of a speeding train with an open channel and an open journal.

There are brochures everywhere, a dart and a map. I hastily pack a few things in a small sack, wave for a taxi and board the train from Penn Station to Boston's South Station. Five hours of transient scenes that could be anywhere in America. Once at South Station, I take the Peter Pan bus to the Steamship Authority ferry terminal in Woods Hole, then set off to the salt marshes of Felix Neck and the surrounding New England sea. I follow the signs to Edgartown, down-island, the place I have chosen somewhat randomly hoping to write, be moved anew. I have a room with a small back porch shaded by surrounding oak trees. There is a lighthouse in the distance that looks as if it was copied from a child's drawing then fashioned in plaster. I optimistically open my notebook on the glass topped desk facing a view of the lighthouse and the winding path that leads to a shallow beach where sailboats sleep on the motionless waters.

Failing to write I decide to explore. I pass through the hall and the outdoor porch unnoticed. In the distance, Chappaquiddick Island, still shrouded in its sad mystery, a drowning girl, a future senator, the last of the brothers. Maybe a little beacon from the children's lighthouse will lead me back to my good thoughts. What if I cut my hair and fast? What if I devote myself solely to my children? What if the world turns in the opposite direction and all trespasses are mended?

I take a walk instinctively following intersecting paths edged with seagrass. There are traces of wetlands, but not as intense or mysterious as those in South Jersey with swarms of gnats, foreboding tall grasses and long-legged insects. The scape is tamer here, but at least a bit familiar. A boat with vertical sails, long black sails, a screaming child, sand and scuff, a marsh too pristine to be a real marsh. I notice the sky is empty. I approach the lighthouse from the back. It is set on a wide base with what appears to be tiles surrounding it. A family gathers before the lighthouse. The father says stand next to Mommy.

*A child lighthouse*

Okay, big smiles, he says. The little girl says, I don't want to be smiling. Why, asks the mother. Because I don't want to be seen in the future with a big smile, she says. She couldn't be more than six years old.

Drawing closer, I discover it to be a replica, a modest monument and spy a plaque, Edgartown Lighthouse Children's Memorial. The tiles are flat stones engraved with the names of departed children. I remain for a while thinking of Stephanie Holt and decide to dedicate a stone in her memory. Perhaps this is why I am here, so that she might join with other children encircling the lighthouse.

Later back in my room I feel overwhelmingly tired. Nonetheless I take my seat at the desk with the glass top to write. A lone mosquito buzzes, brushes my cheek. Don't make me kill you, I say. Again, he hovers around my face with a high-pitched buzzing. Don't make me kill you, I say again, slowly and deliberately. It seems to understand and ceases its buzzing. Most likely we both fall asleep at the same time. A wiry young man riffles through pages of my journal. There are a few blocked paths, he says, let me fix them for you, I'm good at that. It's just a question of clogged arteries, a long equation with aspects left dangling. All right, go ahead, I say, curious to see what he might detect. He reads my pages intently, lightly marking them in pencil.

A dull siren in the distance. I wake disoriented, still at the desk, groggy yet hungry. There is a red light casting from the child lighthouse. One small signal, like a synthetic ruby set in a cosmic ring, the kind of ring one once ordered from the back of a comic book. Slipping out I am startled to see the Milky

Way. The yin-yang moon is cut in half like a black and white cookie. I follow a winding path straight into town. Everything is closing but I find a food stall behind the alley of a kind of shanty shack. Happy with my paper bag of fried clams and cup of black coffee, I sit on a high curb beneath the cookie moon and wonder how I wound up here.

As a young girl I imagined I had come from a nomadic tribe, racing in silent moccasins across a red land in search of alien ships that would touch down and find me, their lost child, and carry me away. Within my father's blood, the hunted and the exiled. And in my mother's blood, the explorer and the huntress. Everything is within us: moccasins disintegrating in my hand, the prayer wheel, shaman bells, reliquaries, goddesses with a thousand arms, the blood that flows through my brother's granddaughter, and the blood of the mind forming these words at this moment.

Dawn breaking. I wind my way back. The winds are high, and I watch the movement of the branches against the pallid sky and the seagrass waving beneath the horizon line. Brice Marden colors, 1971, pale yellow, silvery wind. The boy is within me, as is the mosquito, and the lighthouse, and the memorial stones. I am a fallen one. Not dead, only fallen. Not flung, but blindsided. Not chosen, and perhaps never able to reconcile my trespasses. They cannot be mended; they can only wait for the stitches to dissolve. Over and over, the neglected come to call. Immersed in my own pursuits, my own thoughts, I failed to heed others who have since slipped away.

I miss Sam Shepard. Our long walks, talking endlessly in cafés and playing old blues songs together. We'll limp toward old age together, he promised. I'll pick you up in my truck. We'll go to Mexico and write, two weather-beaten pals. I wanted to tell Sam that I was sorry that I hadn't dropped everything and spent more time with him at the end of his life, but I was too restive, still imagining that we had all the time in the world.

On Down Island I hoped to write. Instead, I experience a succession of infinitesimal raptures, at once a blooming then withering, an inexplicable sorrow relieved by a natural high. What a mind, what a ride we take ourselves on. Telescoping back, I can search for Sam again. I can trace the footprints of my fleeing ancestors, and the Harts possessing the hands of laundresses and shepherds and my mother's mother, sitting on a porch playing her mandolin. We stumble upon a path directing us toward lost loves, a dead child, a necessary stranger. We reach across time for a reassuring hand, a face barely glimpsed, a night of hopeful trials. Keep going, says a voice, tonight is but one night of a thousand to come. Keep going, I repeat entering the diorama of a dream, passing through wrought iron gates of a familiar zoo. I take wide strides hurrying to greet the unattainable, the face of a father never known, imploring him to share his secrets so that I may know the secrets of myself.

3

The gulls of Trieste swoop solo, taunting yet never close enough to satisfy the desire to touch the edges of their chaste wings. How I once dreamed of this place, Trieste, my respective sadness city. I knew of its striking square dramatically facing the Adriatic Sea, the historic Caffè Tommaseo welcoming the writers Svevo and Saba. I knew of the castle on the hill, Rilke addressing the angelic orders, the *Duino Elegies* and the wanderings of Joyce. But I knew nothing of the city's dark crimes, of the Risiera di San Sabba, a looming rice mill that was converted in the fall of 1943, as a transit camp for Jewish prisoners en route to Auschwitz.

It was the sole prison camp in Italy that possessed a crematorium, which the Nazis destroyed along with all damning evidence before they fled at war's end. Yet its breadth can be traced along the brick wall and the confines of a rectangular stain of zinc flooring. Silence mounts in the nearby death stalls and the great hall of crosses. Walking through the narrow entrance of a small gallery I come upon three metal spoons, a pocket watch on a chain with hands cruelly stilled: time frozen at 7:25. A discolored cloth star and two pairs of wire-rimmed spectacles with faded handwritten labels, and purple striped pajamas worn in the nightmare between waking and sleeping.

I feel a heaviness, the same sense of helplessness that I had experienced some years before when visiting the Hiroshima Peace Memorial Museum. Throughout were the humble belongings of victims of the atomic bomb: a charred tricycle, fragments of a coat, a tattered dress, a child's shoe. Nearly the entire city had been incinerated, the present having risen from the ashes. Taking leave, it occurred to me that what truly remained of old Hiroshima was the earth itself, and I knelt and kissed the ground, whispering a plea for forgiveness, for the sake of my father.

I can feel myself plunging like the gulls headfirst into the grainy sea. Everywhere I go seems to bring forth the memory of somewhere else. Nevertheless I pack my few things and bid a hasty farewell to the filmy atmosphere of Trieste and its café lined streets. I board a train to Bologna with its majestic yet crumbling towers and think of Gregory Corso, then to Florence to contemplate the unfinished slaves of Michelangelo, then finally sidetracking to Rome on a small mission.

I read that Gogol spent much time in the Roman atelier of Aleksandr Ivanov, the tortured Russian artist who zealously grappled for nearly twenty years with his massive and strangely obscure painting *The Appearance of Christ Before the People.* I had a strong urge to see the atelier, curious if the aura of his spiritually driven labors yet lingered. I had scrawled a few addresses in my notebook, but the names of pivotal streets had changed. Via Felice, where the Russian painters congregated, now called Via Sistina. There is a memorial tablet to Gogol and a long list of the infamous patrons at Caffé Greco, but I could not find the way to Ivanov's legendary studio with its makeshift scaffolding and wide skylight. Perhaps a ludicrous pursuit, seeking to bathe in the atmosphere of singular obses- sion, a purpose eclipsing all other purposes.

At Tazza d'Oro, a coffee bar near the Pantheon, I stood drinking slowly, reminded of a young painter I sought out long ago, as once again the threads of time insidiously circled my wrist. I was desperately searching for Howard Michels, whom I first met at eighteen, when we were both aspiring art- ists. It was raining and part of his address had streaked and disappeared. After much effort I found his place parallel with the rusted trusses of the deteriorating Myrtle El. He lived alone in an enormous room that seemed to quake as the elevated train passed. We were barely twenty-two. He dried my hair with a stained towel. His canvases reached from floor to ceiling, alluding to de Kooning, yet concurrently casting out the cords of influence. Seeing his work rise above me, I knew in my heart that I would never be a painter; I lacked the muscularity, the physical will. A profound if not scarring breach. I understood in that moment that one must discern between a dream and a calling. I was spun backward, a small child pleading her mother to teach her to read. It was the word that first seduced me and to the word I would return.

We are on this chessboard Earth, we attempt to make our moves, but at times it seems as if the great hand of a disinterested giant haphazardly sends us on a trajectory of stumbling. What do we do? We step back and seek within ourselves what is needed to be done and serve the best we can. I want to write something redemptive, a book like *Pinocchio,* the story of an animated gangling marionette carved by his father, Geppetto. The naughty puppet had an erratic conscience, continually running off, misguided by mischievous influences. Yet in the end he sacrificed himself for the sake of Geppetto. Miraculously absolved, a real boy rose from his lifeless wooden body. Pinocchio found the good in himself and the worth of a father's devotion. I had two fathers, known and unknown, sending signs, feathers falling, gifts of incontestable love.

4

It is an elevated city, the city of emeralds, sitting on a high plateau, Bogotá, the great sprawling capital of Colombia. I fly there for an exhibition and performance at the Teatro Colón de Bogotá, a small jewel of an opera house. I arrive after midnight at the El Dorado airport named after the mythical lost city of gold. Stephan, the creator of Soundwalk Collective, and Santiago, the curator of the Centro Nacional de las Artes, are there to greet me. I feel strangely unbalanced; my heart beats madly and I find myself uncharacteristically out of breath. In the morning the symptoms are joined by a horrendous pounding headache and a doctor is summoned. I am given oxygen and some tablets. It seems that my body is reacting poorly to Bogotá's high altitude. I am obliged to stay on mobile oxygen, rest and hopefully adjust. I mournfully sit propped against the pillow, gazing out my window. Beyond are the cobbled streets of La Candelaria, with its Spanish colonial Baroque and Art Deco architecture, sixteenth-century cathedrals, cafés, and a famous library boasting over two million books.

Everyone visits bringing me herbal remedies, warm corn cakes and coffee from Café Robusta and little gifts, beads and handmade talismans. As the headache subsides, I console myself by reading. Stephan is worried, our performance is tomorrow. I assure him I can do it. Santiago brings books and strengthening teas. He is refined, vigorous. Stephan prepares our installation at the museum; I am left in a warm solitude with the quiet hum of the doctor's machine.

I cannot help feeling a sense of nostalgia, a convalescing would-be traveler with a book upon my lap. In reading Emily Dickinson's *This Is My Letter to the World,* I consider her isolation, her sense of estrangement, an empty mail drop. Her still consciousness her pounding heart. I am overcome with the need to write a letter of my own. But to whom would I write? Perhaps to another age, or a time when we will all be gone. My generation, that is, my ludicrous kind. A letter to those who went to Bible school, who read the classics, who learned to form letters with a dipping pen, who wrote in cursive, who played outdoors for hours unchecked, who slept in the woods and cut their feet on broken glass and told no one. A letter to a distant future, to the ghost of extinct animals, birds, insects, to the empty hives, to the moss-covered cathedrals, to the pulp of knowledge. I will die remembering you, as we are on the brink of losing so much that is precious, moving into a time where a magnificent hologram will replace a forest, where fruit is solely borne on radioactive trees. Where the defaced images of the dictators of our age are plastered on mile long aqueducts and walkways. I am writing to the cows grazing in bright green fields. I am writing to the high white corn, and the tomatoes red and heavy hanging from a tangle of lusty vines. I am writing to the skater unobserved, on a pond of ice melting. I am writing to the sea, to veterans on parade, once proud. To the smelt runs, to hot dogs by the lake, to marshmallows on a stick over the open fire. To skinned knees, flyswatters, skate keys and a bottle of blue Pelikan ink overturned on a schoolgirl's desk.

I dip my pen into a glass inkpot and scrawl these words: I am memory. I am a rabbit, a taxidermy cartoon falling through space. A block of silver burning the fingertips of a grasping child. I am a polished spinet played by the English grandmother who is no longer mine. I am her hand that fashioned lace, her fingers never touched, caresses never felt. I am a knot of hair in my mother's comb. I am ankles, wrists, legs, and arms too long. I am the green couch that opened as a bed. I am the lie that begat another, the blue cornflowers and daisies woven into wilting crowns. I am the arches of my father's feet, the protruding veins of my mother's long legs. I am the terrace of sighs. The gap between sidewalks, prickly weeds, sticky resin, milky sap, honeysuckle, and the hornet whose sting may be counted as a blessing.

A woman brings me warm chicken soup. The kindness of everyone here is humbling. The doctor visits and says I will be able to perform my duties, promising that he will be in the wings with oxygen. But he believes my body cannot truly adjust to the elevation. I think of myself as a child longing to go to Tibet, greeting Sherpas at base camps and turning prayer wheels above the world. The doctor says my condition most likely will prohibit future travel in high altitudes. I am but a swamp and sea level being. Made to gaze up at mountains yet not climb them.

The light recedes in Bogotá. We prevail. I have made new friends I will never see again. I take with me a piece of Bogotá's heart, a small souvenir set in gold, a tiny fragment from the emerald of justice. A fragment as green as the eyes of a mountain I am unable to climb. I send my letter into the air, remembering to show gratitude to nature, to bow my head, to have compassion for those who have not a loaf of bread, nor bed to sleep in, the weary vagabonds who yet somehow find ways to experience the exaltation of existence.

## 5

The last day of the year. My son and daughter and I play music together. My son falls asleep in a chair. The television flickers. There are forty-foot waves on the Pacific Coast. Bethlehem is shuttered. I sit on the sofa with my daughter. The moon is blue, and the light washes over us indigo, sapphire, the color of Fred's birthstone. We are of one mind. Another year closes. My daughter Jesse is beautiful yet does not know it. My son weaves fretworks of melodies he does not remember. I feel a sudden wave of regret. If only to be swept back through time, my children in my arms, back to our yard with the blue pickup truck the pear tree and their sleepy-eyed father at the screen door.

The captain of our little boat with one blue sail set out without me. He was my Captain, and our boat was like the doves setting out alone together, further and further away, always to return. With a poem, with a piece of music, with a child, and with another. Now I walk by the sea, back and forth just as I once had done but with no song, only words. Not even words spoken or written, words murmured, drowned by the insistent waves. Like Mrs. Muir, trying to remember, walking through life, alone so it seems, until the appointed time when the ghost of her Captain will be waiting.

He is also here, and we are waltzing on that highway, as the cars speed by and the stars emerge, one by one, twinkling their approval. He smiles that smile, the one that says we are the same, we still have it. I look around, and no one has noticed, and I go on my way, shaking my head, back in so-called real life. That is what I live for, the mist of his return. He reaches across the realms, all the worlds of the divine comedy, all stages of human transformation, all dust of things and all I need to do is hold my breath and believe and he is there for a moment, an hour, a shudder, in a vast ballroom lit by the icy tail of a shimmering comet.

6

In *Sun and Steel* Yukio Mishima speaks of the lust for ascension. It is encased in his poem *Icarus.* Perhaps he is speaking of the lust for illumination, possibly the artist's greatest sin. Like the architects of Babel attempting to reach the realm of God, to penetrate and bathe in it, eat of it. Not satisfied with the beauty of the natural world, the artist seeks the unnatural kingdom, the kingdom of the mind, plucking from higher realms and revealing the components of Cubism, or the notes of an unfathomable fugue. In this way, one could say that Eve, seeking knowledge, was potentially the first artist. And what did she create? The good of Abel, the evil of Cain. There is magnificence, and there is magnificent failure. Perhaps that is what drew Mishima to Icarus, the hubris to challenge the Sun. The artist seeks paradise in life, he seeks what must not be sought.

We race after the sun. The pen ceases its scratching. A curtain of forest velvet falls, a welcoming glow draws me to my worktable. I will finish what I started in Nice, in the Hotel Suisse, where James Joyce first envisioned *Finnegans Wake,* the incomprehensible tome that opened the twentieth century. It was also my century. At times I mourn the worlds I knew, the

*Bay of Angels*

hopes of my generation, flowers in hair, dancing to The Dead, seeking a universal music, "the language of peace," as Jimi Hendrix would say. These thoughts pass through as a version of a Brahms lullaby plays in the café's sound system. It begins and blends with mournful carols, all written with great hope and jubilation that when slowed down feels dirge-like as if in a pasture dotted with sheep who have lost their shepherd.

—Do you believe in us, they ask.

—I believe in everything. I smile.

I believe my mother will find her mother and three lost sons in paradise. I believe my sister will walk upon the soil of the New World. I believe in the parallel mind that has a parallel mind of its own. I believe in my own myths, the lines and arrows on childish charts of forgotten lands once designed by my own small hand. I believe they exist, these places, found, lost then revisited, whose shining edges wane, then curiously return, as a silken boomerang.

Memory restores and winds through the veins of a shredded map. I found my voice through my travels. My singing voice, my writing voice. I had traveled through eastern Europe and ended in Poland in a place called Charlotty, with its strange forest, and one small zoo guarded by an old Mongolian camel with a shaggy coat, two humps and long lashes framing his big sad eyes. I wanted to write there, but I couldn't and found myself despairing, haunted by the porcelain face of a doll who sees all but offers nothing. I had finished my tour with the band, and a friend suggested I join him in Nice in a hotel overlooking the Bay of Angels. My room was small and flooded with light. There was a table and chair set on the balcony overlooking the bay. It was overcast but I could see the sun gathering strength behind a silvery veil, soon to be pierced. But at that moment it was the perfect light to photograph, everything below had the appearance of a nineteenth-century rotogravure. But I no longer had a camera. My notebook and pen yet dormant. I watched the veil, now pierced, split and slip away. Unconsciously, I began to write and then kept writing through the afternoon.

It occurred to me that Joyce sat on a similar balcony overlooking the same bay; I felt a wave of conspiratorial joy. In the coming days I sat in the early mornings and twilight time, and I wrote. Words poured before me. I heard them in my head, then watched them form as if from another source. The weather turned, and the rain and high winds kept me from the balcony. What does it all mean I wondered but kept writing. My right eye experienced shooting pains, bits of electricity, but I could not stop writing, imagining I possessed the gift of some Joycean energy. But it was not James Joyce I was accessing, it was the great wake, the concentrative energy of a new idea emerging. It was all flowing, a mental current circulating in the corridors. It was a night and another night hammering, words that might someday beget a book.

In those days I fell in love with the Hotel Suisse and the circular view of the Bay of Angels, the place where drought was relieved by a sudden torrent of words opening all wounds. The place where the rebel hump rose from the waters like the fin of an ancient amphibian. I focus on calm blue waters, where a boat drifts, one that has drifted for eight hundred years, holding the remains of a very small saint, with dainty hands and feet. I notice revolutions in the sky, wooden ships, wheels, and dismembered hands turning. The reality is the rain and the wind, a few pages of notes that will hopefully find their way into something greater. I wear a hooded cloak of an oil-skin well worn, irresistibly light. I travel like Gogol by coach into a blackness not known before, save by myself, the blackness of ink filling a glass bottle. I can do as I like with these thoughts, these wild parallels, without knowing if the rising sign in the bay reflects a regenerated giant or the golden mound of a disinterested camel or the return of some mythological creature, some misanthropic mutated alien with the silver blood of elves and fairies. I squat with my siblings before an old bureau, slowly turning the loose dresser knobs. We pass trees of great height, deep green firs and head boldly into dark skies etched with bright clouds. Rainbow weather! I cry out, as we follow ships with billowing sails and conquistadores on horses with heavy silver saddles.

Suddenly I am on my own in the center of a miraculous storm. Let it come! Replenish our rivers and let us cast nets beneath the sturgeon moon, the color of a small girl's bonnet. Pools in the red earth form a healing clay that I scoop up to cover my face and hair. There is pelting hail. I lose my shoes and perhaps my way, but no matter. There are makeshift maps flitting above me, revealing ridges of unknown continents and strange islands inhabited by equally strange animals with claws and scales and wide hollow nostrils. *Rebel hump rebel hump, tramping through the reeds, the uncompromising ferns, sidestepping the stinkweed and swarms of gnats.* Barefoot, I follow streams laced with algae and rushing tadpoles, on alert for the glint of a coin, a prodigal penny, the shard of a mosaic, or the hand mirror of oneself.

In a certain way I have not changed so much. But the incandescent restlessness has somewhat quelled and a sense of all the things I have loved are so deeply absorbed that I can project *Guernica* without seeing, hear *Ascension* and My Bloody Valentine without listening, leaf through *The Glass Bead Game* without reading, feeling them with all my being. All must fall away. The precious bits of cloth folded away in a small trunk like an abandoned trousseau, the books of my life, the medals in their cases. Shedding is one of life's most difficult tasks. One by one we apportion our talismans. But I will keep my wedding ring and my children's love.

In the shedding what remains is honor. We evolve, we falter, we learn from our transgressions, and then repeat them. We plunge back into the abyss we labored to exit and find ourselves within another turn of the wheel. And then having found the fortitude to do so, we begin the excruciating yet exquisite process of letting go. There is a brilliant calm, akin to natural light. All about us is debris, and yet we step lightly so not to tread a waning silhouette, our own primordial skin.

What aspect of being shall I present? One with a thundering step gathering imagined troops, one that joined the brethren to call out against the tyranny of governments, false prophets, politicians, and profiteering poets. Or perhaps one who had a succession of loves, or who possesses a black velvet case containing the pearls from a beloved husband. Or the child who recited Scriptures yet stole from her father's pockets and lied to her mother. We all harbor our own set of scales. The checks and balances of life is every human's secret.

What is blood's currency weighed against the needs of a hungry child? Where do our efforts fall on the scales of worth? The scroll unwinds, the angels guide my little boat. I drag a net and haul away the cast-off coat, skin, loves, dying cells from the tides of the water body. I see myself on that same balcony of the Hotel Suisse, just a writer on holiday, dressed in white, gazing intently upon a triangular speck in the center of the bay. The vague itch returns. What shall I write of and what shall I vow? I promise to be good. I will write of a young girl who finds a small hand mirror lying in the grass. She signals to that speck, so far away and yet so very close. She joyfully leaps, suspends mid-air, then touches down with arms outstretched. Welcome, rebel hump, she cries, I am you.

ABOUT THE PHOTOGRAPHS

The author gratefully acknowledges the following photographers for use of their images:

page 63 © Linda Smith Bianucci
page 90 © Lynn Goldsmith
page 110 © Frank Stefanko
page 116 © Frank Stefanko
page 146 © Jody Caravaglia
page 152 © Seiji Matsumoto
page 183 © Judy Linn
page 194 © Steven Sebring
page 198 © Annie Leibovitz
page 223 © Melodie McDaniel
page 277 © Lisa Marie Smith

Above: Steven Sebring, St. Clair Shores, 1995
Frontispiece: Peter Pan, Kensington Gardens, Patti Smith
Pages 156, 168, 172, 178: photographs by Fred Sonic Smith
Pages 173, 247, 250, 262: photographs taken by the author

## ABOUT THE ARCHIVES

Photograph of my parents with Toddy on the green brocade couch taken by Bobby Williams in 1951.

All vintage images, on pages 8, 18, 208, 214, 241, photographers unknown, are from the Smith family archive, courtesy of my sister, Linda Smith Bianucci.

My mother, Chick Kaven, and Dot Ashman, page 228, and poem "Patti" page 242, are from my baby book.

Young Fred with his grandfather Herbert Bias, page 122, from the private family archive of Fred's sister, Pat Hallett.

The sole wedding photograph, page 160, was taken in the Mariners' Church by Fred's mother, Kathleen Bias Smith.

Thanks to Lenny Kaye and Andi Ostrowe
for providing invaluable material from
their personal archives.

Patti Smith is the author of the National Book Award winner *Just Kids,* as well as *Woolgathering, M Train, Year of the Monkey,* and *Collected Lyrics.* Her seminal album, *Horses,* has been hailed as one of the top 100 albums of all time. Her global exhibitions include Strange Messenger, Land 250, and Camera Solo. In 2005, the French Ministry of Culture awarded Smith the title of Commandeur des Arts et des Lettres. Inducted into the Rock & Roll Hall of Fame in 2007, Smith is also the recipient of the ASCAP Founders Award, Sweden's Polar Music Prize, and the 2020 PEN/Audible Literary Service Award. In 2022, Smith was named Officier de l'Ordre national de la Légion d'honneur, France's highest order of merit.

A B O U T   T H E   T Y P E

This book was set in Granjon, a modern recutting of a typeface produced under the direction of George W. Jones (1860–1942), who based Granjon's design upon the letterforms of Claude Garamond (1480–1561). The name was given to the typeface as a tribute to the typographic designer Robert Granjon (1513–89).

*Family, Central Park, 2019*